THE WORD FOR THE WISE

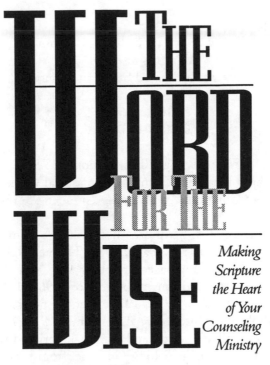

THE WORD FOR THE WISE

*Making
Scripture
the Heart
of Your
Counseling
Ministry*

HENRY BRANDT, PHD
& KERRY L. SKINNER

FOREWORD BY HENRY T. BLACKABY

BROADMAN
& HOLMAN
PUBLISHERS

Nashville, Tennessee

4262-76
0-8054-6276-7

Dewey Decimal Classification: 253.5
Subject Heading: Counseling \ Pastoral Work
Library of Congress Card Catalog Number: 95-15676

Unless otherwise noted, Scripture quotations are from the New King James Version, © 1979, 1980, 1982, Thomas Nelson, Inc., Publishers. Other versions used are the NASB, New American Standard Bible, © the Lockman Foundation, 1960, 1962, 1963, 1968, 1971, 1972, 1973, 1975, 1977, used by permission; the NIV, Holy Bible, New International Version, © 1973, 1978, 1984 by International Bible Society; and Phillips, reprinted with permission of MacMillan Publishing Co., Inc. from J. B. Phillips: The New Testament in Modern English, rev. ed., © J. B. Phillips 1958, 1960, 1972.

Library of Congress Cataloging-in-Publication Data
Brandt, Henry.
    The word for the wise : making Scripture the heart of your counseling ministry / Henry R. Brandt, Kerry L. Skinner.
      p. cm.
    ISBN 0-8054-6276-7
    1. Counseling—Religious aspects—Christianity
    2. Counseling—Biblical teaching I. Skinner, Kerry, 1955–
II. Title.
    BR115.C69B73   1995
    253.5—dc20

                          95-15676
                          CIP

99 98 97 96 95 5 4 3 2 1

Contents

Foreword by Henry T. Blackaby   vii

Preface   xi

Acknowledgments   xvii

1. Portrait of a Biblical Counselor   1
2. Attitude Toward Trouble   22
3. The Sinful Nature   33
4. Methods of Counseling   49
5. Counseling Distinctives   74
6. Counseling in the Body of Christ   94
7. The Role of Repentance in Counseling   107
8. Feeding on the Word   119
9. Teach Me to Grieve   133
10. Adultery   151
11. How to Deal with Anger   161
12. Deceit and Hypocrisy   190
13. Humanism   209
14. Truth, Professionalism, Servanthood   215

Appendix: Listening Sheet   235

Foreword

Here is a book I wish had been available when I began my ministry in California thirty-seven years ago. I have been involved in biblical counseling throughout my ministry—I still am! My phone constantly rings when I am home, and people seek me out when I am on the road. Leaders, including missionaries, are always asking me how I find real and lasting answers to my needs, the needs in my family, and the needs of those whom God has placed in my care. Sunday School teachers, business leaders, teenagers, college students—all want practical answers to their most pressing problems.

The first twelve years of my ministry were in California, during the tumultuous 1960s. In the first five years I conducted more than three hundred funerals and ministered to the bewildered and grieving with their endless and painful questions. I sat with the widows and orphans and led them to God's sure provisions for their lives. I watched as God met their needs. He faithfully showed Himself real, personal, and faithful in His promises. I was their shepherd, leading them to their Lord, who loved them, young and old alike. I counseled with criminals and gang members as well as police officials.

As I was confronted with deep pain and bewilderment in those who came to us, I always *knew* beyond doubt that

God had real, practical, and healing answers for any need that anyone might face.

Prayer, to me, was always God's invitation to seek *His face* and to receive from Him! I cannot, to this day, recall any time He was unfaithful! However, I always *began with Him*—that He is God, He is Truth, He is Love, and He is Sufficient! I then asked Him to

1. help me understand and trust Him as He revealed Himself to me in His Word;
2. help me obey what He showed me, by His Spirit;
3. enable me to live my faith in Him authentically before others in my personal life, my family, and as a shepherd of His people;
4. help me faithfully shepherd His people to know and experience Him and His provisions for their lives.

God heard and responded, and He continues to do so to this very day.

However, during these years I watched, with amazement, many sincere leaders, teachers, pastors, and ordinary believers turn to the world and its promises. In doing so, many forsook turning to God. The world does not have an answer for sin! Therefore, these believers came up empty and broken. Often I watched with great sorrow as God's people suffered greatly. The world's counselors could comfort, relieve, and even help them cope, but could not *heal*. Only God can heal! Their counselors in the world were often like the "blind leading the blind," for the counselors often had problems as deep, if not deeper, as their counselees.

The message of this book is real, practical, true, and greatly refreshing. Dr. Henry Brandt and Kerry Skinner tell the Truth as expressed by God in His Word. They give great practical help for anyone who seeks to help others through personal and corporate counseling. They define the problems in the counseling process accurately. They are faithful to God's Word, in their own witness and in their teachings. This is a much-needed prophetic voice for our day. Both are like sought-after friends who are found. This is especially true for pastors and other leaders who have burdened hearts (and often wounded hearts) for God's people today!

This book is sounding an urgent call: God's people, personally and together, forming God's provision for helping the broken and confused to come to Him for forgiveness, healing, and restoration. God's leaders must return to

1. the Bible for clear guidance from Him;
2. a clear and biblical diagnosis of the problem in people's lives as God reveals it—sin;
3. the teaching of repentance for God's people;
4. a faithful shepherding into Christlikeness—God's goal and promise for everyone who will believe Him;
5. the encouragement of churches to seek the corporate healing within the body of Christ, with Jesus as the Head, directing and enabling them.

I pray that all who read this "call" to authentic biblical counseling will find new enjoyment and victory in placing their lives alongside the broken and bewildered.

Henry T. Blackaby

◆

Preface

I became a Christian in my early twenties. My drinking and carousing days ended abruptly, and my life was centered in church and parachurch activities. Over a period of several years my interest in these activities gradually faded.

In 1942, at age twenty-six, my background was serious frustration with my work, my marriage, and my social life. I was struggling to contain a very angry, hostile response to my situation. Finally, I turned to Christ and asked Him to be the Lord of my life and help me. Almost overnight I repented of my anger, had calmed down, relaxed, and began to enjoy life—the very life I previously could not endure.

People noticed the change and asked me if I could help them. I found myself attracted to their needs.

A group called VCY (Voice of Christian Youth) felt responsible to share the news of Christ with young people. The backbone of the program was a monthly youth meeting, where a speaker would tell the audience about Jesus and give opportunity for anyone to come and talk to a counselor about their needs.

My only qualifications was that I cared about these people. They had all kinds of personal, interpersonal, and family problems. There was much anger, confusion, hatred, and other issues raging in these young people. I had no training, no biblical knowledge, and no experience. But I cared. I would go home and, with the help of a Bible concordance, begin to build up some biblical information about sin, repentance, and the work of the Holy Spirit. The Bible began to come alive.

I struggled with my new information. There was no one to turn to while I listened to these young people and adults pour out their frustrations. As best I could, I would try to use my meager knowledge about how God will help.

You may be longing to be helpful to someone. You tell yourself you have no training, no experience, no biblical knowledge, and no contacts. You can ask God to send someone along who needs to know what knowledge you *do* have of God. The Lord will show you how to use it.

We learned that the Bible introduces us to a God whose power gives us everything we need for life and godliness (see 2 Pet. 1:2–4); it provides a basis for judging the thoughts and intents of the heart (see Heb. 4:12); it is useful for teaching, rebuking, correcting, and training in righteousness (see 2 Tim. 3:16). People can approach the Creator of this universe and Savior of the world for help.

> Now we have received not the spirit of the world, but the Spirit who is from God, that we might know the things that have been freely given to us by God. These things we also speak, not in words which man's wisdom teaches but the Holy Spirit teaches, comparing spiritual things with spiritual. But the natural man does not receive the things of the Spirit of God, for they are foolishness to him; nor can he know them, because they are spiritually discerned.
>
> 1 Cor. 2:12–14

Since I chose to accept Jesus as Lord in 1942, I have had people seek me out to tell me their troubles. What they called "trouble" in 1942 has not changed to date. The range can be described by using six Bible verses—three quote Jesus, and three quote Paul:

"For from within, out of men's hearts, come evil thoughts, sexual immorality, theft, murder, adultery, greed, malice, deceit, lewdness [lust] envy, slander, arrogance, and folly. All these evils come from inside and make a man 'unclean.'"

Mark 7:21–23, NIV

The acts of the sinful nature are obvious: sexual immorality, impurity and debauchery; idolatry and witchcraft; hatred, discord, jealousy, fits or rage, selfish ambition, dissensions, factions and envy; orgies, and the like.

Gal. 5:19–21, NIV

All of these are called sins in the Bible. Treatment is to turn Godward and repent; that is, agree with God that it is sin, ask for forgiveness and cleansing, and then walk in the Spirit which is given to us.

The fruit of the Spirit is love, joy, peace, longsuffering, kindness, goodness, faithfulness, gentleness, self-control.

Gal. 5:22–23

There is a gulf fixed between looking to the world or to God for relief and strength. Sincere, dedicated people stand on both sides of this gulf. Many people seek to straddle the gulf hoping to benefit from the best of both worlds.

One way to describe the two worlds is that on one side people experience a cure by looking to God to cleanse them from sin and empower them to walk in the Spirit. On the other side people experience great relief by learning to live with, or manage, their sins.

A competent therapist who says there is no God and no sin is skilled at helping people draw upon normal self-control, loyalty, determination, and intelligence to channel anger, hate, and self-will into constructive channels. To be able to manage such emotions and urges is a great relief. This can be done without giving God a thought.

The biblical counselor's purpose is to help persons discern if their lives fit with biblical principles. Deviation from those principles is called sin. There is no human remedy for sin. Help is out of this world, but it is immediately available to those who meet God's requirements. The strength to live in the Spirit is also out of this world, but it is also available on demand on a day-to-day basis.

There is relief available on both sides of the gulf. What difference does it make which side relief comes from? Jesus offers an answer:

> Peace I leave with you. My peace I give you; not as the world gives do I give to you.
>
> John 14:27

The rest of this book chronicles our journey in search of a biblical knowledge of God.

Henry Brandt

A major spiritual marker in my ministry occurred when I attended a *MasterLife* workshop in Houston, Texas, in the early 1980s. My stale personal walk with God was challenged, corrected, and converted to a deep, fresh, daily encounter with God.

Discipleship has been the central point of ministry for my wife and me since those days. God's Word has given direction for many personal and corporate decisions. In the four churches I served, many people's lives were changed through discipleship courses such as *MasterLife* and *Experiencing God.* I noticed, however, that people in discipling groups were not excluded from crises. Times of crisis provide practical times for applying God's Word to life.

First Baptist Church of West Palm Beach, Florida, was a very special place that God allowed me to serve. There God taught me more about biblical counseling. Our pastor invited Dr. Brandt to share with the staff how God had taught him the difference between "relief" and "cure" as it related to counseling.

Relief is good but it is not a cure. If sin is your problem, there is no human remedy for sin. As I learned from Dr. Brandt, I noticed that what he was sharing and what God had taught me through the years began to flow together. I always seemed to know that the Word of God had direction for every area of life, but I was not clear in how to share the Word with a hurting person.

How could I help people? I had undergraduate and graduate degrees, but my training was not in counseling. I learned that people could be helped when led to encounter God. Since then, God has taught me much about how to use His Word to help Christians. The answer to people's problem is simple; the process is not always easy.

God's way is not our human way. Helping people does not depend on intellectual skills, academic degrees, or experience. These are great resources, but they are empty apart from the Holy Spirit and God's Word. Before serving churches, I thought my training would make the difference between success or failure in ministry. However, through fifteen years of studying God's Word in a personal relationship with Him, I discovered my confidence came from the *truth* of God's Word. If His Word was truth, I knew I could share it. If I could share it, He would use the Word to change the hearts of His people.

Simplicity is the key word in biblical counseling. Our world seems complex. Paul stated,

> But I fear, lest somehow, as the serpent deceived Eve by his craftiness, so your minds may be corrupted from the simplicity that is in Christ.
>
> 2 Cor. 11:3

If there is simplicity in Christ, it is available to any Christian.

There is room for the professional counselor and the lay counselor in the body of Christ. Both, however, must use the Bible as the source of help if they are to be called "biblical." While I was not trained academically and clinically as Dr. Brandt was, he and I found that God is powerful enough to use anyone who loves God, loves His Word, and loves His people.

Many with less training than I have led people with failing marriages, poor self-esteem, and sinful attitudes to God's answer—Jesus. May I encourage you to "be diligent to present yourself approved to God, a worker who does not need to be ashamed, rightly dividing the word of truth. . . . useful for the Master, prepared for every good work" (2 Tim. 2:15, 21).

Kerry L. Skinner

◆

Acknowledgments

In 1992, God directed Henry Brandt to write materials that would help meet the needs of hurting people in our congregation. We soon realized that when God speaks through His Word, He gives truth that set people free. This truth needed to be shared with others.

God stimulated us to produce the manuscript. He gave us wisdom, strength, and daily guidance to share how He would meet the needs of His people. The Word of God was central in leading us to share how "His divine power has given to us all things that pertain to life and godliness" (2 Pet. 1:3, NKJV).

We spent much time with our pastor, Keith Thomas, and associate pastor, Mike Shepherd, struggling with how to meet the needs of so many. Henry Blackaby encouraged us to stay with the assignment.

Henry's wife, Jo, kept encouraging him to make good with his end of the work.

My wife, Elaine, gave encouragement and much prayer support.

Many have helped, but to God be the glory for revealing His answer for life needs.

Henry Brandt and Kerry L. Skinner

◆

1

Portrait of a Biblical Counselor

The basic requirement for a biblical counselor is character, not academic training. Paul taught Timothy how to be "approved to God, a worker who does not need to be ashamed, rightly dividing the word of truth" (2 Tim. 2:15).

Four Character Qualities of a Biblical Counselor

God gave Paul a portrait of a servant who wants to help others, a biblical counselor:

> And a servant of the Lord must not quarrel but be gentle to all, able to teach, patient, in humility correcting those who are in opposition, if God perhaps will grant them repentance, so that they may know the truth, and that they may

come to their senses and escape the snare of the devil, having been taken captive by him to do his will.

2 Tim. 2:24–26

Four character qualities identify a biblical counselor:
1. The Lord's servant does not quarrel.
2. The Lord's servant is gentle to everyone.
3. The Lord's servant is able to teach.
4. The Lord's servant gently instructs opponents.

God's Word gives no greater description of the character of a biblical counselor than in 2 Timothy. A further look into 2 Timothy 2:24–26 reveals these qualities.

Characteristic 1: The Lord's Servant Does Not Quarrel

In those early days I occasionally found myself arguing with people who disagreed with my witness. Usually I won the argument but lost the person. This is an example of the Bible coming alive. This verse was a rebuke to me and caused me to pray for grace not to argue.

I also learned that I needed to consciously and knowingly build a relationship with Christ by studying His Word and practicing the principles that I find there. I must be an example of one who is enjoying the benefits that come from following the Master.

Reviewing my interactions with people and my reactions to them helped reassure me that I was appropriating the resources available to me from God. As it was written,

Let all bitterness, wrath, anger, clamor, and evil speaking be put away from you, with all malice. And be kind to one another, tenderhearted, forgiving one another, even as God in Christ forgave you.

Eph. 4:31–32

Two Bible verses caught my attention early on:

I have learned in whatever state I am, to be content.

Phil. 4:11

and,

Let the peace of Christ rule in your hearts, . . . and be thankful.

Col. 3:15, NIV

These verses spoke to me because I struggled with a vicious temper. Repentance rather quickly changed me to taking more and more incidents contentedly and peacefully that normally would have made me furious. As a result, I began identifying easily with unhappy people. Perhaps this is why people would come to me when they were upset, even when I was in my infancy as a Christian.

My own experience helped me understand that God would help me to be content in any circumstance. By faith, I would tell people that God would help them go through their experience contentedly and peacefully. I became increasingly confident in the truth of Philippians 4:11 and Colossians 3:15. I saw people with all varieties of experience allow the Lord to comfort them.

There is another incredible verse:

Praise be to the God and Father of our Lord Jesus Christ, the father of compassion and the God of all comfort, who comforts us in all our troubles, so that we can comfort those in any trouble with the comfort we ourselves have received from God.

2 Cor. 1:3–4, NIV

Characteristic 2: The Lord's Servant Is Gentle to Everyone

A sense of personal control, quietness underneath your skin, and joyful and hopeful perseverance is evidence of good spiritual health.

Therefore, having been justified by faith, we have peace with God through our Lord Jesus Christ, through whom also we have access by faith into this grace in which we stand and rejoice in hope of the glory of God. And not only that, but we also glory in tribulations, knowing that tribulation produces perseverance; andperseverance, character; and character, hope. Now hope does not disappoint, because the love of God has been poured out in our hearts by the Holy Spirit whom was given to us.

Rom. 5:1–5, NIV

For this very reason, make every effort to add to your faith goodness; and to goodness, knowledge; and to knowledge, self-control; and to self-control, perseverance; and to perseverance, godliness; and to godliness, brotherly kindness; and to brotherly kindness, love. For if you possess these qualities in increasing measure, they will keep you from being ineffective and unproductive in your knowledge of our Lord Jesus Christ.

2 Pet. 1:5–8, NIV

This gives you the ability to quietly handle pressure, perplexities, persecutions, rejections, and suffering when you experience:

- a dirty trick
- a crisis
- financial pressures
- death

Enjoying a problem means:

- blood pressure—normal
- muscles relaxed
- breathing easily
- digestion good
- emotional calm
- mind at ease

You need to watch yourself grow in grace and in the knowledge of the Lord Jesus Christ. Then you can reassure others that God's Word is true.

Growth in grace, peace, joy, love, comfort, and knowledge, and growth in the ability to deal with people without hypocrisy and partiality are basic to a growing confidence in God's Word as a sure Guide for yourself and others. When your advice contradicts your life, the bloom of life is gone. Spiritual fitness cannot be stored. Neglecting spiritual fitness is a self-inflicted risk. A counselor who loses his or her temper, or has pouting spells, or is dishonest, or who is tense, anxious, worried, fearful, hostile, or temperamental obviously is not experiencing the fruit of the Spirit. However, that person knows how to repent, receive forgiveness, be cleansed, and renewed.

Characteristic 3: The Lord's Servant Is Able to Teach

The Lord's servant must be sure about his knowledge, fluent about his knowledge, and familiar with his knowledge. In 1942 I discovered these verses:

Above all, you must understand that no prophecy of Scripture came about by the prophet's own interpretation. For prophecy never had its origin in the will of man, but men spoke from God as they were carried along by the Holy Spirit.

2 Pet. 1:20–21, NIV

The word of God is living and powerful and sharper than any two-edged sword, piercing even to the division of soul and spirit, and of joints and marrow; and is a descerner of thoughts and intents of the heart.

Heb. 4:12, NIV

All Scripture is given by inspiration of God, and is profitable for doctrine, for reproof, for correction, and for instruction in righteousness, that the man of God may be complete, thoroughly equipped for every good work.

2 Tim. 3:16–17, NIV

Well of Wisdom. One of my goals has been to plumb the depth of the riches found in Romans 11:33:

> Oh, the depth of the riches both of the wisdom and knowledge of God! How unsearchable are His judgments and His ways past finding out.

The Bible becomes a living book. I found that once I committed to serve the Lord He showed me how to use the truth of His Word to help people. As I did this, not without fear and trembling, the Bible became more alive. As my understanding of God's Word kept enlarging, so did my sphere of witness. People began to seek me out for help with their troubles.

Character Development. What the people we worked with really longed for, whether they knew it or not, was what the Bible calls the work of the Spirit of God. We developed a list of some of the qualities available from God by request if sought after on God's terms. This list is a summary of six Bible verses.

Hope ✦ Compassion ✦ Considerateness ✦ Wisdom
Joy ✦ Endurance ✦ Submissivness ✦ Kindness
Peace ✦ Patience ✦ Merciful ✦ Faithfulness
Comfort ✦ Love ✦ Impartiality ✦ Gentleness ✦ Grace
Purity ✦ Sincerity ✦ Self-Control ✦ Goodness

(Rom. 15:13; 2 Cor. 1:2–4; Col. 1:11; 1 Thess. 3:12; James 3:17–18; Gal. 5:22–23)

Characteristic 4: The Lord's Servant Gently Instructs Opponents

The servant of the Lord gently instructs those who oppose him in the hope that God will grant them repentance, and lead them to a knowledge of truth, and that they will come to their senses and escape from the trap of the devil.

You cannot shove God's comfort down unwilling throats. I have watched some people with amazement who would become as disturbed and inconsolable over the loss of car keys as others are over the loss of a family member.

It has been especially rewarding to see people who faced death—either their own or someone they knew—reach out and receive comfort and forgiveness that God offers so freely. On the other hand, many bereaved people are unconsolable. I would offer these verses to bereaved people who faced the death of a family member who would not be comforted. The inevitable question would come, "Have *you* ever lost a family member?"

"No," was my weak reply, "but I have observed many others whom God comforted when they let Him."

"That's easy for you to say," is often the response.

It seemed logical that broader experience would give me more credibility. My mother died when I was forty-two years of age. Nine years later my father died. In 1982, my wife died after a long, long struggle with cancer. In 1986, my second wife died suddenly. I have experienced many different kinds of disappointments.

Why do I tell you this? Because I have learned that my experience or faith in God made known through the Bible meant nothing to anyone who for whatever reason refuses to be comforted.

Meeting God on His Terms

My experience has confirmed *for me* that the Bible, which I accepted by faith in 1942, is trustworthy. The Bible does not need my experience to make it more credible. It does not need any opinion polls or research projects.

Anyone who approaches God must meet *His* conditions:

Without faith it is impossible to please Him, for he who comes to God must believe that He is, and that He is a rewarder of those who diligently seek Him.

Heb. 11:6, NIV

We are His witnesses. We know that God is trustworthy because we took a step by faith and our experience confirms our choice. For anyone to discover this trustworthiness for themselves, they must begin at the starting line—by faith.

"Enter by the narrow gate; for wide is the gate and broad is the way that leads to destruction, and there are many who go by it. Because narrow is the gate and difficult is the way which leads to life, and there are few who find it."

Matt. 7:13–14, NIV

Christ's Ambassadors to Needy People

Helping someone with a spiritual need became and continues to be the delight of my life. As I look back now I recognize that my efforts to help people grew out of my own hunger to know God and to serve Him.

Eventually I went on to college and university to earn academic degrees. I learned that it is not academic degrees that empowers a person to serve God.

We are ambassadors for Christ, as though God were pleading through us: we implore you on Christ's behalf; be reconciled to God. For He made Him who knew no sin to be sin for us, that we might become the righteousness of God in Him.

2 Cor. 5:20–21, NIV

We can speak on Christ's behalf. A small group of us called Voice of Christian Youth (VCY), accepted that challenge. As we did, the Bible became more and more alive. Like Paul, we realized:

> I am obligated both to Greeks and non-Greeks, both to the wise and the foolish. That is why I am so eager to preach the gospel. . . . I am not ashamed of the gospel, because it is the power of God for the salvation of everyone who believes.
>
> Rom. 1:14–16, NIV

Then, too, we began to sense another truth:

> Christ's love compels us, because we are convinced that one died for all, therefore all died. And he died for all, that those who live should no longer live for themselves but for him who died for them and was raised again.
>
> 2 Cor. 5:14–15, NIV

Looking back on those beginnings in VCY, we realized that the love of God in us is what caused us to respond to people in need.

There are needy people all around us today. Are you aware of them yet feel inadequate for lack of training? Perhaps the Lord is beckoning to you to let Him use you to give spiritual help to people around you.

We need to remind ourselves we speak in Christ's place and use His words. The counselee is dealing with God. If we do our part in the Spirit, the result is between the counselee and God—not eloquence or charm; not education; not technique or manner; not presentation.

Mr. Mix

Frequently in counseling, you will be challenged. For example, a pastor was dealing with a member of his church who was having marital difficulties. This member—we will call him Mr. Mix—was very active in Christian service, spending four or five nights each week at the church. Finally his wife came to the pastor in an appeal for help. She claimed that her husband came to the church so much because they were not getting along. He was mean to the children. He would beat them so hard that welts would rise on the skin. Though he worked at the church, he refused to finish the addition to the house that he had started. These were a few of her many grievances.

The pastor asked Mr. Mix to come and see him. He told Mr. Mix of the conversation with his wife—and Mr. Mix became furious. When he cooled off, the pastor said, "Let me read you some Scripture."

> You are still worldly. For since there is jealousy and quarreling among you, are you not worldly? Are you not acting like mere men?
>
> 1 Cor. 3:3, NIV

Mr. Mix blew up and shouted, "Do you mean to tell me that you would act differently if you were in my position?"

What would you answer if you were asked a question like that? Your reaction at such a moment in counseling is crucial. If you have confidence in God's Word and are growing in Christ, you can be calm and assured rather than anxious and frustrated.

The pastor quietly reminded Mr. Mix of God's resources, available to him whenever he was ready to receive them. Mr. Mix stormed out of the study, but did not shake the pastor's confidence in the Bible any more than the refusal of a patient to fill a prescription would shake a physician's faith in medicine. Later Mr. Mix came back for help because of the example of the pastor. If the pastor had not been living in the Spirit, he might have ended up in an angry shouting match. If so, he would need to practice what he preaches—confess, repent, receive forgiveness, cleansing, and renewed strength.

Misery of Her Own Making

Another pastor was faced with a mother whose daughter had eloped with a man of another ethnic group. She blamed herself and was utterly miserable. The pastor told her she need not be in misery. Her reply was, "What? You expect me to be happy with such a problem in my family?"

This was a touchy situation. Here was a woman who came to him in search of peace. When he told her she could be comforted, she was even more upset. Actually she wanted to find a way to break up the marriage; she refused to be comforted unless this was done. The pastor pointed out that comfort comes from God and that she should commit this problem to Him rather than take it in her own hands and insist on her way.

The pastor patiently and firmly showed her that her misery was her own making and that God would give her peace if she asked. The pastor was not afraid to present the truth even though it upset her. Of course the truth hurts—much like the surgeon's scalpel. But following God's Word is the only way to peace.

This pastor could firmly guide this woman into heeding the Scriptures because of his own confidence in God and his own Christlike, Spirit-filled life. He had no reason to be shaken when she got upset and angry. He knew he had good news for her. He was certain that God could help her and give her peace because he was experiencing God's peace. Though he had not faced an identical problem, he had faced other problems and knew firsthand the comfort of the Lord in contrast to the futility of self-inflicted pity and misery. As a result, the woman went away with her burden lifted.

People usually defend themselves if they are wrong. The counselor attempts to clarify the issues, but will not argue or quarrel. Often it is not easy to distinguish between searching and quarreling. The difference between resistance and rejection, between generating heat or light, is difficult to determine. It is easy to confuse firmness with a lack of love.

How do you demonstrate a gentle, kind, loving spirit? By agreeing? By keeping your opinion to yourself? Gentle firmness can be interpreted by the counselee as being blunt, hard, or unsympathetic, especially if you challenge their reasons for their symptoms.

The biblical counselor needs to continuously check up on his own spiritual life to be prepared to respond in the Spirit to the occasional surprise response of a disturbed counselee.

"You Do Not Believe Me!"

On one occasion a man and his wife came for counsel from a long distance. They had driven six or seven hours and had planned to stay with us for several days. We were chatting amiably (I thought) for a few minutes before going to our rooms. The lady began giving me a well-rehearsed list of reasons why her tension was the result of events in her past history. After listening for ten minutes, I offered what I considered some hope. I asked if she would consider looking into the Bible with me so I could show her that her past experiences cannot block the peace of God from calming her down.

In a high-pitched voice she screamed, "You do not believe me!" She ran into a bedroom and screamed like a frustrated child.

Her husband reassured me that I observed a *mild* version of her response to being crossed.

Situations like this are examples of uncontrollable hostility, and they require a kind, gentle, patient response. This particular woman packed up and left.

A Strange Way of Clearing His Throat

A newlywed came to see me. Her husband annoyed her so much she could hardly stand being in his presence. What could cause such distress in a brand new marriage?

She and her husband married after a whirlwind courtship. She had known him only four months. After their marriage, she discovered that he had an annoying way of clearing his throat every five minutes or so. She asked, "How can I tell my husband without upsetting him?" She thought if she could get him to stop doing that, she would be her sweet self again. I advised her to be alert to other sources of irritation now. Could she recall some irritations in her past associations?

She returned with a long list of irritating people in the past and the present. Her husband's strange way of clearing his throat faced her with her sinful nature. Perhaps her husband should change because his strange way of clearing his throat was socially unacceptable. However, it would not solve her problem with a sinful nature. She had been plagued all her life with hatred, discord, anger, and selfish ambition. She did not know that these were sins.

I could have listened to her story from a humanistic view. We could have devised a way to inform her husband about his wife's problem. In fact, we did so. He was eager to help. The annoying condition was eliminated, and she was relieved. Wonderful. It is true that we could have given her relief without giving God a thought. But, if we only changed the environment, she would be back because somebody or something else would irritate her.

She was ready to see that she had two problems to solve:

1. Her husband's habit
2. Her irritability

Only God could help her with her irritability, which was really her sins. Upon receiving Jesus into her life, then she could partake of the fruit of the Spirit daily.

Relief or Cleansing?

Some of the most miserable people I know are Christians. So it is not to say that a person who confesses to be a Christian is a person who is facing himself as he is and taking his problems to God.

You can make adjustments apart from God that will make you comfortable. It is like living with a sore thumb. The first day you will hit it a few times. You will soon learn to keep it out of the way. People have, so to speak, sore thumbs. If they avoid certain people or circumstances, or refuse to get involved in certain conversations, they will avoid discomfort.

We can learn to live comfortably with our sin by avoiding those circumstances that would stir it up. You will calm down. You may have too much pressure on your job. Get a job with less pressure and things will improve. If you get out from under these circumstances, your condition will not be evident. It will be there, but it will be dormant. If the reason for the pressure was rebellion, the pressure will return when you are asked to do something you do not want to do. The cure for rebellion is to turn to God to cleanse your heart. However, relief from rebellion can come by changing jobs.

Who Must Change?

A young woman has habits that disturb her mother. Both are Christians. The mother keeps insisting that her misery is caused by her daughter's behavior. Accordingly, the mother feels quite certain that the solution to her problem is to change her daughter. Further, this woman believes she should not be agreeable toward her daughter lest she seem to be giving her blessing upon her daughter's unacceptable habit. She is being a good Christian, she thinks, by being angry and impatient with her daughter. She does not even want peace. She feels that a good mother should be miserable when her daughter is not behaving herself.

She has two problems. One is her inner reactions to her daughter. Once she gets those straightened out, then and only then is she ready to deal with her daughter's behavior. The daughter should be corrected for her own sake, because her behavior does not conform to God's Word. There are two separate circumstances here.

The woman needs to help her daughter see herself as she is for her sake. As a counselor, I help the mother see herself as she is for her sake, not because growth makes me happy. If I were to depend on the company I keep for my happiness and joy, I would be one of the most miserable people of all!

The Biblical Counselor's Source of Joy

The Lord's servant needs time to stay healthy. What the athlete does to stay healthy is done alone. No one else can do it for him. The results will show up in the game. What the servant does to stay spiritually healthy is also done alone. No one can do it for you. A regular routine is helpful so you have a basis for judging your spiritual health.

One day I was listening to the recital of problems and ills for thirteen hours. I enjoyed it only because my joy does not come from what I listen to; my joy comes from God. So congenial companions are not necessary for you to be joyful. I help people for their sakes. I must do it from a joyful heart myself.

Repentance or Sorrow?

To help a person examine himself in the light of the Bible is hard to do. It is so easy to quote the verse,

> If we confess our sins, He is faithful and just to forgive us our sins and to cleanse us from all unrighteousness.
>
> 1 John 1:9

I find that people shrink away from this kind of confession. Repentance is rare. Jesus warned:

> "Now, you Pharisees make the outside of the cup and dish clean, but your inward part is full of greed and wickedness. Foolish ones! Did not He who made the outside make the inside also?"
>
> Luke 11:39–40

So our behavior, our thoughts, feelings, desires, actions, and speech must be identified in detail and dealt with separately.

Many people insist that a period of depression or self-condemnation or sadness or remorse or weeping is evidence of repentance. It is not necessarily so. I encounter people who are very sorry because they got caught lying, or misbehaving, or gossiping, or cheating, or whatever. To be sorry because they got caught and to be repentant is not the same thing.

Counselees will often resist facing themselves and ask, "Is it good for me to look into my heart? Isn't it better to just wipe the slate clean and look forward?" I think the Bible tells us quite clearly,

He who covers his sins will not prosper, but whoever confesses and forsakes them will have mercy.

Prov. 28:13

A very important step for the counselee is the confession and acceptance of his behavior for what it is. To find the peace and joy that we are looking for, we must first of all recognize those things in our lives that need to be confessed and forsaken. It is important for us to admit to God, "Yes, I am that way. No excuses, no alibis; I am that way and I am sorry." People who approach God on this basis are people who are well along the way to tapping the source of peace and joy that is available through God.

Focal Points

- Character is more important than academic training. Character, goals, love, and knowledge of the Bible are basic.

- Diagnosis is tough. It is what exists! It must be accurate!

- The counselee may direct his sin at you—our Lord was abused, despised, rejected, and eventually crucified.

- The style of counseling grows out of the counselor's character and attitude.

- Your job: Get the counselee headed in right direction.

Physician vs. Biblical Counselor

One of the most honored and respected of all the professionals is the physician. But in many ways, the biblical counselor is a specialist on the same level. The eternal destiny of the counselee may be at stake. This is a far greater issue than the physical or mental health of the counselee.

Medical Specialist—Physician	Biblical Counselor
1. Trained to work from a norm.	1. Trained to work from a norm.
2. Standard equipment: stethoscope, blood pressure equipment, thermometer, scale, syringe.	2. Standard equipment: the Bible.
3. Pokes, probes, and pricks you, draws blood and samples of body excretions, makes you swallow strange-tasting stuff, uses x-rays and other strange machines, incise, etc.	3. Asks personal, strange questions.
4. Asks personal questions, information includes medical history, but they focus on present condition.	4. Information includes past history, but they focus on present condition.
5. Friendly, kind, gentle doctor—patient tends to become anxious, apprehensive, embarrassed.	5. Friendly, kind, gentle. The counselee tends to be anxious, apprehensive, embarrassed. Truth is hard to handle, no matter how gentle the counselor is.
6. Diagnosis depends on condition of the body and the physician's medical knowledge.	6. The diagnosis depends on the condition of the counselee and the counselor's biblical knowledge.
7. Patient may resist diagnosis—refuse treatment. This definitely is not a social call.	7. Counselee may resist diagnosis—refuse treatment. Definitely not a social call.

Your specialty is a comprehensive knowledge of the Bible and absolute confidence that it is God's sure guide for all people. When you preach, teach, or counsel, you stand straight and talk in the confidence that you are the custodian of the most important information in the world.

Gordon Harmon, in his article, "Evangelical Principles and Practices" (*Christianity Today*, XI:13, Jan. 2, 1967), wrote:

> The believer also learns by experience that the Bible, welcomed in the heart, brings faith, peace, and triumph in his life; and neglected, means failure and sin. He finds promises that, trusted in, beget assurance; commands that, obeyed, produce the beauty of holiness; warnings that, heeded, save him from folly and sin; principles that, applied, give wisdom how to act; passages of praise and prayer that, appropriated, are a source of needed inspiration.

You may look to other disciplines for help in perfecting your interview technique in counseling, developing your skill to listen objectively, or learning how to help the individual tell his story. But your view of the nature and needs of people is to be drawn from and is to coincide with God and His Word.

Definition of a Biblical Counselor

What is a biblical counselor? A biblical counselor will be referred to as any person (pastor, teacher, husband, wife, friend, etc.) who uses the Word of God as the foundation for sharing truth with a person who needs to "escape the corruption in the world caused by evil desires" (2 Pet. 1:4, NIV).

Why is it important to center the foundation on "the divine nature" (2 Pet. 1:4)? God's Word is truth. The mind of man can give human reasoning and solve some human problems, but only divine wisdom (God's Word) will have solutions to "evil desires."

Will people always desire to be comforted in their troubles? No. Some who come to you may be ready for repentance and life change. Others will simply want a counselor to console, sympathize, and agree with their condition. Remember, you can not shove God's comfort down unwilling throats.

Can your experiences shed light on God's Word? No, but God's Word will shed light on your experiences. For example, one does not need to experience murder to know it is wrong, or know joy is good without experiencing it. How? Simply by reading, studying, and living in a relationship with Jesus as the Scriptures share:

> How unsearchable are His judgments and His ways past finding out!
>
> Rom. 11:33

If a person wants to become a professional counselor there are certain academic studies and an internship period required in order to be licensed. The biblical counselor may or may not meet such academic qualifications. The basic requirements are not academic; they are personal characteristics:

- A joyful, relaxed wholesome attitude toward life
- A Spirit-filled person who looks to God for wisdom and discernment
- One who loves to encounter God through studying His Word on a regular basis
- One with a reputation for good judgment in interpersonal relations, marriage and family relations, finances, and helping people—based on biblical knowledge
- One who loves to help others apply God's Word to life

If a biblical counselor were to have received a letter from the apostle Peter, it would sound like an accurate summary of the work of a biblical counselor.

To those who have obtained like precious faith with us by the righteousness of our God and Savior Jesus Christ: Grace and peace be multiplied to you in the knowledge of God and of Jesus our Lord, as His divine power has given to us all things that pertain to life and godliness, through the knowledge of Him who called us by glory and virtue, by which have been given to us exceedingly great and precious promises, that through these you may be partakers of the divine nature, having escaped the corruption that is in the world through lust [evil desires].

2 Pet. 1:1–4

Take a closer look. A knowledge of God leads to predictable results:

- Can distinguish right from wrong

- Has an abundance of faith, grace, and peace

- Gives us everything we need for life and godliness

- A way of escape from corruption in the world caused by evil desires

It is not surprising that our politicians, our educators, and even many ministers have lost the basis for spelling out a code of ethics or morals. Rather than looking to God for guidance, the prevailing mood is to banish His Word, the Bible, as a source that gives us direction.

◆

2

Attitude Toward Trouble

What attitude should a biblical counselor have toward the difficulties, problems, tensions, fears, and worries of other people? We face our own problems in a certain way and tend to recommend the same procedure to others.

I was talking to a minister this morning who sympathizes with people who are disgruntled because they live with a grumpy, complaining mate. He thinks they are justified in feeling sorry for themselves under circumstances like that. He himself is discontented and lives with a grumpy mate, so his expectation for someone else is the same as his own experience. But experience is not a safe guide—God's Word is. Consider what a Christian's heart can be:

> You will keep him in perfect peace, whose mind is stayed on You, because he trusts in You.
>
> Isa. 26:3

Warning Signs

Pain in the body is a warning that cannot be ignored. Pain demands our attention. It warns us that the body is not functioning properly. Likewise, restlessness, anxiety, worry, and tension that cannot be explained by a physical problem should warn you that something is disrupting your peace. Has your mind drifted away from steadfast trust in God? The body is warning you that your relationship with God needs some attention.

Many people do not want to hear this. This is especially true of persons facing a troublesome problem. Most people discuss their problem with someone else before they come to a counselor. They may have been reassured that their lack of peace is normal under the circumstances. They expect sympathy. They expect the counselor to accept their reasons for their lack of peace.

Counselees are often convinced that the story they tell is unique, but the counselor has heard the same theme again and again. You know that peace of heart is just a prayer away. If there is a predictable time when your judgment will be received gladly, I have not found it.

"I Am Your Problem"

Many people do not even want peace in their circumstances. A mother was at odds with her teenage daughter, a senior in high school. The girl made her miserable and angry. The mother was telling me how terrible this girl's behavior was. I asked her, "What does your daughter do?" She could not think of anything. "I just cannot seem to think right now, but my daughter sure is a problem."

"Tell me about some of the problems," I said. Again, "I just cannot think," was her reply.

I suggested to this mother that, rather than her daughter not liking her, maybe she does not like her daughter. She was horrified at a thought like that. "I love my daughter with all my heart." This woman became disgusted with me. She wanted to be comforted under her pesent circumstances.

Her response was, "What? You are just like the rest of them. I thought when I came in I would have someone who would understand me. But you do not understand me either."

She took out her checkbook. Tears dropped down on the check. I said, "Wait a minute. You had better come back." What a way to treat a mother in that spot! Was I hard, harsh, and heartless? That wrung my heart, but counseling breaks your heart. I did care. Should I have withheld my opinion for another session?

When this mother returned home from my office, her daughter asked in a belligerent kind of way, " I suppose he said that I am your trouble, right?" The mother said to her daughter, "That is what I tried to get him to say, but he would not say it. He said *I* am your problem."

Our attitude toward the people we deal with is important. We must face them as gently and kindly and patiently as we can with the truth. But let us not tamper with the truth. The daughter's behavior did not cut off the mother from the peace of God. There must be something else in the picture. I advised the mother to come back. She was not sure. Just because people do not like my advice does not worry me. She came back. There was more to her story.

Her husband had died eight months before. She lived next door to his mother, and she began trying to boss her mother-in-law. Her husband's grown children from a former marriage disagreed with the way she handled their mother. Everyone was against her. Should the counselor sympathize with the lady? We often equate kindness with untruthfulness. To say what you think will soothe her, whether it is true or not, is not being kind.

This mother had a serious problem. After she gave me this additional information, she said, "Look, I came back to tell you that you are wrong. You told me I did not like my daughter. I watched this week, and I am convinced more than ever that my daughter does not like me."

I said, "You do not need to defend yourself. Why are you so anxious to convince me that you love your daughter? I think you are bitter and resentful." In fact, she was.

Sooner or later you must get to the heart of the problem. Instead of people walking out of your office happier than they were when they came in, they may walk out of your office more miserable. Many times you will need to help people see that their sin is bigger than they thought it was.

If your attitude toward the person you are dealing with is to make this person feel better no matter what, then you will minimize the person's sins. They will be relieved for the moment, but you will not be much help in the long run.

I urged this mother to make another appointment to see me. She stormed out of the office, but she came back the next week.

She said, "This week the Lord spoke to my heart, and I can see my antagonism where I work. I have come to realize how hostile I am toward my child. I have been bitter and rebellious against God. I have repented, and I have peace."

She changed, but her situation did not change. When you need peace, you must go to the source. The source of peace is not in a change of circumstances; the source of peace is God. He can comfort you in tribulation. She had not wanted to be comfortable in her tribulation. She had blamed her sins on the circumstances. Since then she has brought her daughter to see me.

Speaking the Truth in Love

How should the counselor respond to the counselee's impassioned description of the cause of their misery? We must listen "in the Spirit." This means a gentle, kindly, patient spirit. You are listening for some violation of a biblical principle. We cannot tamper with the truth. What has drawn this person away from peace?

The biblical counselor must "speak the truth in love" (Eph. 4:15). This verse does not address the timing for telling the truth. When to declare the truth is a matter of judgment. Should it be in this session? Should it be in another session?

People who come for help are disturbed, broken, hostile, angry, and jealous. You are not doing any favor by saying, "There, there, there! I understand. Anybody in your position would feel the way you do." That is cruelty. The best news you will ever tell anybody is that there is peace, joy, strength, and grace sufficient for the day. If the counselor gives an illustration of God's sufficiency, the counselee often resists receiving that help from God. This still amazes me. John 3:19–20 speaks to this issue:

> "And this is the condemnation, that the light has come into the world, and men loved darkness rather than light, because their deeds were evil. For everyone practicing evil hates the light and does not come to the light, lest his deeds should be exposed."

People do not want to be evaluated. Why? Because of their evil thoughts, evil words, or evil deeds. The counselor must expect people to dislike having their deeds brought to light. They will hate it, but the counselor must take a long look at it, trying to put this person in touch with the Spirit of God.

Surgery hurts. The surgeon will cause you excruciating pain in order to eliminate pain. Does that make sense? Yes, of course. Sometimes you are willing to risk your life to have an operation because you want to get better. The counselor must keep the goal in mind, not just how a single counseling session comes out. As I reflect on a session, my concern needs to be that my heart is right.

Freedom from Bitterness

I have a counselee whose husband walked out on her. She has four children and is left to care for them round the clock. Her husband does not help support the children. If that woman is to find any peace, she must find it in that situation. He has since divorced her. If she has any hope of joy, she must find it where she is.

Her question: How would you react if you were me?

Answer to question: You are asking about a hypothetical situation. Paul wrote some of the most helpful letters while he was in the stocks in prison with the festering sores of the whip still healing.

Imagine this mother with her four children. If she is to enjoy life, it will be under those circumstances, tied down twenty-four hours a day. She is in a tough spot, but she is managing. She argued with me, "You do not understand. You have never had to take care of four children like I have. You do not know what my husband was like."

I do know what God is like. I do know that His grace is sufficient for my own troubles, and there is no use telling you about my troubles.

My task was to help her recognize that she was bitter. I had to help her find freedom from her bitterness. How would she deal with her marriage and parental problems once she was free from her bitterness? She was smart

When someone tells us that we do not understand what a certain situation is like we must respond that we know what God is like enough to figure that out. She was trying to get away from the need to confess her own sin. You cannot see straight or think straight if you are out of step with God.

Shepherding or Counseling?

Your ministry will take on a new authority once you reach the conviction that God is sufficient for all needs. You need the backdrop of successful interaction with people—joy in your own life when trouble comes. You are learning that you can be of good cheer in troublesome times.

The fruit of the Spirit is available in troubled times. Sometimes pastors must call on church members who are taken in a fault—experiencing a marital or family crisis, a financial crisis, or bereavement. It may be a very tense, highly volatile atmosphere. How do you handle counseling situations like that?

I would not call these counseling situations. In counseling, persons choose to come to you. They choose the reason. When you call on a member, I would call that shepherding. You may or may not be welcome.

Preparation is important. Consider this verse:

> Brethren, if a man is overtaken in any trespass, you who are spiritual restore such a one in a spirit of gentleness, considering yourself lest you also be tempted.
>
> Gal. 6:1

This only applies to those who are spiritual. What is the fruit of the Spirit? Love, joy, peace, gentleness, kindness, goodness, patience, faithfulness, and self-control. If you qualify, then go to that person and offer shepherding. If you do not qualify, take care of your own problem first.

You do not make a shepherding visit to look down at anyone. You are going to an equal who has the same potential as you. Why does Paul say, "you who are spiritual"? Because when you go to someone who is taken in a fault, the person will probably tell you to mind your own business. You are apt to feel the same way about that person. This is flesh arguing against flesh, and you will get nowhere that way. When the person's flesh is directed against you, your response needs to be in the Spirit.

"I Can't Understand the Bible"

Often people insist that the Bible is hard to understand. If so, I ask about their reading level in other areas. Can they understand the newspaper or textbooks? If they can absorb information in other areas, I try to help them see that they are resisting the God of the Bible. I do not believe the Bible is that complicated. People who have trouble with the Bible are not really interested in living by it. They may not have a personal relationship with Christ. I reassure people how simple the Bible is. They do not need to study Greek or go to seminary to comprehend the Bible. Anyway who wants to please God can understand His Word.

Lately I have been absorbed with Paul's prayer to the Colossians:

> strengthened with all might, according to His glorious power, for all patience and longsuffering with joy.

Col. 1:11

I have been applying this prayer in counseling situations.

A lady comes to me whose husband is a problem drinker. As I ask her questions, I find how disgusted and angry this husband makes her. I turn to Colossians 1:11 and ask her to listen. "Strengthened with all might [she is already nodding!], according to His glorious power, for all patience and longsuffering with joy."

She says, "Yes, isn't that wonderful?" I ask what the verse means. She does not know, and she does not want to listen.

"When do you need patience?" No answer.

"Specifically when do you need patience?"

"I suppose when my husband is drunk," she replies.

"Yes, that is true. Are you willing to be patient with your husband when he is drunk?" Often the answer is no.

"What is the source of joy according to Colossians 1:11?" She could not think. "It is very simple. The source of joy is God's glorious power. You need God's power most when your husband is drunk and mean."

People rarely like that kind of advice. But they may never see any change until they can be joyful during times of trouble.

"It's hopeless. How can I have any joy when he is drunk?" This is resistance. She does not want to face up to her own angry loathing toward him.

Next I may try another verse:

> Now may the God of hope fill you with all joy and peace in believing, that you may abound in hope by the power of the Holy Spirit.
>
> Rom. 15:13

What is the source of hope? You just read it. God. What is the source of joy? God. I see many hopeless people who face hopeless situations. My advice to those people is, "You are not hopeless because you are in that situation. You are hopeless because you are out of fellowship with God. You are out of touch with the source of hope."

The woman with a drunken husband has a problem with him. But before she can deal with her problem, she must deal with herself. I prefer to say that the Bible is simple and to the point. People can understand Romans 15:13 if they have a mind to please the Lord.

Common Questions

What about Prayer?

Question: Will you pray with me?

Answer: Of course I will pray with a counselee; however, I think it is important to make it clear that I am not a mediator between them and God. I cannot do their confessing, or repenting, or yielding, or surrendering for them.

Occasionally people return saying, "Your prayer did not work." But did they do what they agreed to do? Or did they stop doing what they agreed to stop doing? Often they were not praying with me as I prayed for them. I tell them that if it is sin that needs attention or if it is the fullness of the Spirit that is needed, they must deal with God alone.

What about Victory?

Question: Do you always have victory in your life?

Answer: At the point where I become conscious of lacking victory in my own life, I must practice what I preach or my ministry will start going downhill. There have been times when I have rebelled against being victorious.

I know of a person who needs to do certain things in his relationship to his wife. I have been telling him he is a rebel. When will he get rid of his rebellion? When he wants to, that is, when he is willing to be free from it. People often enjoy being rebellious; they are very reluctant to give up the flesh and pleasures of sin. If you pin people down, they will admit they like to have fights.

I sometimes counsel young people about sex. When it comes right down to it, they do not want to yield their bodies to God. They like the thoughts that go through their minds. What they really want to know is how they can keep these thoughts and not feel so miserable about it.

This struggle against the sin in our lives is not easily set-tled. When you deal with sin, you are in a battle. Many counselees will refuse to abandon their sin. So do not be concerned if you are not particularly "successful." You can help people go through the rituals, but they will keep on in their sin. This is hard for the counselor to accept.

There is great temptation to go with the flow. The bibli-cal counselor quickly realizes that he or she is headed upstream. Here is a reminder when you get a cool response to the good news:

> Our eyes fixed on Jesus the source and the goal of our faith. For he himself endured a cross and thought nothing of its shame because of the joy he knew would follow his suffer-ing; and he is now seated at the right hand of God' s throne. Think constantly of him enduring all that sinful men could say against him and you will not lose your pur-pose or your courage.
>
> Heb. 12:2–3, Phillips

◆

3

The Sinful Nature

The word *sin* has almost disappeared from our vocabularies. Most of us do not know how to define the word. There is no human remedy for sin. The only source of instant cleansing from our sins is Jesus Christ.

The Good News of Christ

When Jesus was born, an angel of the Lord said,

> "And you shall call His name JESUS, for He will save His people from their sins."

Matt. 1:21

The best news ever announced was by a host of angels who appeared to shepherds tending their flocks, saying:

"Glory to God in the highest, and on earth peace, goodwill toward men!"

Luke 2:14

The living Savior died to make it possible for us to find a source of peace for our own hearts and to give us goodwill toward all the people who have sinned against us.

After the crucifixion, Jesus' disciples gathered in a room with the doors locked. They were filled with fear. Jesus appeared in the middle of them. He said:

"Peace to you! As the Father has sent Me, I also send you." And when He had said this, He breathed on them, and said to them, "Receive the Holy Spirit."

John 20:21–22

My mind races to a description of the work of the Holy Spirit in our lives. The Spirit produces fruits such as these: love, joy, peace, patience, kindness, generosity, fidelity, tolerance, self-control (see Gal. 5:22–23, Phillips).

Before Jesus ascended to heaven, He gave His disciples a twofold directive:

[1] "Repentance and remission of sins should be preached in His name to all nations."

Luke 24:47

(I like the Phillips translation of the same verse: "So must the change of heart which leads to forgiveness of sins be proclaimed in his name to all nations") and

[2] "Teaching them to observe all things that I have commanded you; and lo, I am with you always, even to the end of the age."

Matt. 28:20

What Is Sin?

We are to finish the work that God sent Jesus to do on this earth. Jesus came to save us from our sins. It is our responsibility to make sure that this tiny word *sin* means what God wants it to mean.

It is personal sin that separates us from God.

> Behold, the LORD's hand is not shortened, that it cannot save; nor His ear heavy, that it cannot hear. But your iniquities have separated you from your God; and your sins have hidden His face from you.
>
> Isa. 59:1–2

A biblical counselor needs to have a working knowledge of the definition of sin and be comfortable about passing that knowledge on to the counselee. The next few pages describe sin. This will not be pleasant reading. The counselor must have a knowledge of this dark side of life in order to diagnose sin.

> Whoever commits sin also commits lawlessness, and sin is lawlessness.
>
> 1 John 3:4

Illustrations of Sin

There is no human remedy for sin. Immediate supernatural help is available. The following runs the gamut of what counselees present to me.

Jesus said,

> "What comes out of a man, that defiles a man. For from within, out of the heart of men, proceed evil thoughts."
>
> Mark 7:20–21

Jesus then lists thirteen items that proceed from the human heart:

- evil thoughts
- adulteries
- fornications
- murders
- thefts
- covetousness
- wickedness
- deceit
- lewdness
- an evil eye
- blasphemy
- pride
- foolishness

And even as they did not like to retain God in their knowledge, God gave them over to a debased mind, to do those things which are not fitting.

Rom. 1:28–31

Paul lists twenty-one items that are "not fitting" (see vv. 29–31). These words describe what is happening in our world today. Note the reason why it is happening!

- sexual immorality
- wickedness
- covetousness
- maliciousness
- full of envy
- murder
- strife
- deceit
- evil-mindedness
- backbiters
- haters of God
- violent
- proud boasters
- inventors of evil things
- disobedient to parents
- undiscerning
- untrustworthy
- unloving
- unforgiving
- unmerciful

What are the acts of the sinful nature? Paul presents a list of seventeen items in Galatians 5:19–21.

- adultery
- fornication
- uncleanness
- lewdness
- idolatry
- sorcery
- hatred
- contentions
- jealousies

- outbursts of wrath
- selfish ambitions
- dissensions
- heresies
- envy
- murders
- drunkenness
- revelries

You were taught, with regard to your former way of life, to put off your old self, which is being corrupted by its deceitful desire.

Eph. 4:22, NIV

Paul gave the Ephesians a list of nine items to "put off" (see vv. 25–31):

- falsehood
- stealing
- unwholesome talk
- bitterness
- rage

- anger
- brawling
- slander
- malice

Please study these other Scriptures:

But if you show partiality, you commit sin, and are convicted by the law as transgressors.

James 2:9

Therefore, to him who knows to do good and does not do it, to him it is sin.

James 4:17

All unrighteousness is sin, and there is sin not leading to death.

1 John 5:17

These six things the LORD hates, yes seven are an abomination to Him: a proud look, a lying tongue, hands that shed innocent blood, a heart that devises wicked plans, feet that are swift in running to evil, a false witness who speaks lies, and one who sows discord among brethren.

Prov. 6:16–19

He who despises his neighbor sins; but he who has mercy on the poor, happy is he.

Prov. 14:21

The devising of foolishness is sin, and the scoffer is an abomination to men.

Prov. 24:9

But the wicked are like the troubled sea, when it cannot rest, whose waves cast up mire and dirt. "There is no peace," says my God, "for the wicked."

Isa. 57:20–21

"For rebellion is as the sin of witchcraft, and stubbornness is as iniquity and idolatry. Because you have rejected the word of the LORD, He also has rejected you from being king."

1 Sam. 15:23

This is certainly not an exhaustive list. But you have just completed a list based on only twenty-eight verses. Is it not strange that a word that is so central to the reason why Jesus came to this earth has all but disappeared from our vocabulary?

The Spirit-Filled Life

A biblical counselor needs to know how to lead the counselee into a Spirit-filled life. These verses mirror that life, yet only reflect a tiny glimpse of the Spirit-filled life.

In Romans 15:13, Paul prayed that God would fill the Christians with three items:

joy • peace • hope

In Galatians 5:22–23, the apostle discusses the fruit of the Spirit by presenting a list of nine items:

* love
* joy
* peace
* longsuffering
* kindness
* goodness
* faithfulness
* gentleness
* self-control

Paul lists four virtues in Colossians 1:11–12 (NIV), after praying that the believers would be "strengthened with all power, according to his glorious might":

* great endurance
* patience
* joy
* thankfulness

In Colossians 3:12–17, Paul instructs the believers to "put on" twelve virtues:

* tender mercies
* kindness
* humility
* meekness
* longsuffering
* bearing with each other
* forgiveness
* love
* the peace of God
* thankfulness
* letting the word of Christ dwell in you
* gratitude

James 3:17 lists eight items in speaking of "the wisdom that is from above":

- pure
- peaceable
- gentle
- willing to yield

- full of mercy
- full of good fruits
- impartial
- without hypocrisy

Please study these Bible verses:

I know how to be abased, and I know how to abound, Everywhere and in all things I have learned both to be full and to be hungry, both to abound and to suffer need. I can do all things through Christ who strengthens me.

Phil. 4:12–13

For he who fears God will escape them all.

Eccl. 7:18

The fear of the LORD leads to life, and he who has it will abide in satisfaction; he will not be visited with evil.

Prov. 19:23

We that are strong ought to bear with the failings of the weak and not to please ourselves. Each of us should please his neighbor for his good, to build him up.

Rom. 15:1–2, NIV

With all lowliness and gentleness, with longsuffering, bearing with one another in love.

Eph. 4:2

Pleasant words are like a honeycomb, sweetness to the soul and health to the bones.

Prov. 16:24

Better is a dinner of herbs where love is, than a fatted calf with hatred.

Prov. 15:17

These Bible verses give us a glimpse of the work of the Spirit—a tiny glimpse, as you can see in the chart on the next page.

This chart puts the contents of these verses together. You can use it like you would a mirror.

As you scan the right-hand column, a Bible verse becomes very meaningful:

No man can justify himself before God by a perfect performance of the Law's demands—indeed it is the straight-edge of the Law that shows us how crooked we are.

Rom. 3:20, Phillips

As you scan the left-hand column, another Bible verse becomes meaningful:

Live by the Spirit, and you will not gratify the desires of the sinful nature.

Gal. 5:16, NIV

The apostle Paul writes that the entire law can be summed up in one single command:

"You shall love your neighbor as yourself."

Gal. 5:14

How Must We Treat Sin?

Treating sin involves teaching the listener the basics of confession, repentance, cleansing, and yielding to the Holy Spirit.

Self-Help

Today's massive emphasis on human help interrupts and interferes with the Good News. Human help will enable

Spirit-Controlled Living vs. Sin-Controlled Living

Spirit-Filled Mind		Sins of the Mind	
forgiveness	humility	unforgiveness	pride
hope	thankfulness	evil thoughts	ingratitude
appreciation	confidence	covetousness	selfish ambition
willingness	wisdom	greed	deceitfulness
impartiality	faithful	lust	heartless
self-control	gratitude	arrogance	faithless
merciful		senseless	haughty
		despiteful	

Spirit-Filled Emotions		Sinful Emotions	
love	joy	hatred	anger
peace	longsuffering	rebellion	unloving attitude
gentle spirit	kindly spirit	bitterness	jealousy
gladness	patient	envy	malice
	compassion	bad temper	rage

Spirit-Filled Mouth		Sins of the Mouth	
truthfulness	praise	lying	slandering
thankfulness	timeliness	complaining	disputing
gentle answer	soothing tongue	yelling	backbiting
encouraging	pleasant words	contentiousness	quarrelsomeness
tact		boasting	blasphemy
		gossip	

Spirit-Filled Behavior		Sins of Behavior	
kindness	gentleness	fornication	brutality
righteousness	self-control	adultery	without self-control
obedience	cooperation	drunkenness	stealing
goodness	sincerity	murder	violence
courage	servant	revelry	disobedience to
endurance	submissive	insolent	parents
considerate	impartial	ruthless	brawling
		factious	favoritism

you to live with and manage a sinful heart. Teaching, training, and therapy can help you be aware of unwholesome attitudes, evil thoughts, and stirrings of emotions so that you can redirect them constructively, drawing upon your willpower and determination.

Several methods of self-help can be beneficial: Supervision and accountability, support groups, behavior modification, setting goals, a carefully administered drug program.

Welcome relief from the effects of a sinful heart is available without giving God a thought. Helping people find relief from the effects of their sinful hearts is creeping into the churches of our nation.

You may ask, "What is wrong with relief?" Nothing is wrong with relief as long as you recognize it as relief. The bad news is that human relief is a massive barrier that interferes with our sense of need for a Savior.

God's Help

Several Bible verses point to God's help—the supernatural way—to change the sinful heart.

> "If you openly admit by your own mouth that Jesus is Lord, and if you believe in your own heart that God raised him from the dead, you will be saved."
>
> Rom. 10:9–0, Phillips

> If we freely admit that we have sinned, we find him [God] reliable and just—he forgives our sins and makes us thoroughly clean from all that is evil.
>
> 1 John 1:9, Phillips

> And not only that, but we also glory in tribulations, knowing that tribulation produces perseverance; and perseverance, character; and character, hope. Now hope does not

disappoint, because the love of God has been poured out in our hearts by the Holy Spirit who was given to us.

Rom. 5:3–5

The Spirit produces fruits such as these: love, joy, peace, patience, kindness, generosity, fidelity and self-control. There is no human source of such qualities. They are freely available to anyone who has received Jesus Christ as Lord. The key is to

live by the Spirit, and you will not gratify the desires of the sinful nature.

Gal. 5:16, NIV

You will become gentler, kinder, more patient, more generous and able to manage your urges so they satisfy you and the people around you. Isn't that what you are looking for?

The Seriousness of Sin

Sin should be taken at least as seriously as AIDS. The Bible tells us that Jesus is seated at the right of God's throne. I can picture Jesus observing us. We have elevated all sexual activity to the level of normal, expected behavior. The only condition is to practice safe sex. AIDS is transmitted primarily by unsafe sex. What is Jesus thinking when He watches the antics of intelligent, educated people?

Jesus must be wondering when we will dust off three ancient rules that would eliminate AIDS:

1. Avoid sexual immorality (see 1 Thess. 4:3).
2. Do not commit adultery (see Mark 10:19).
3. Whoever looks at a woman to lust for her has already committed adultery with her in his heart (see Matt. 5:28).

This caution ought to be posted in every school and public building:

Therefore he who rejects this [abstinence from sexual immorality] does not reject man, but God, who has also given us His Holy Spirit.

1 Thess. 4:8

Jesus said that sexual immorality, lust, and adultery are sins against God. How do you curb sexual immorality? It is only sin. No human help or effort will do the job. But Jesus will save us from our sins.

The urge toward sexual immorality is, humanly speaking, all but unmanageable. It is a ticket to AIDS and a dozen lesser venereal diseases, unwanted pregnancies, broken marriages, shattered families, destroyed reputations. Worst of all, it is a sin against the living God.

Think of it. The spread of a horrible international disease could be wiped out if we would call sexual immorality what Jesus called it—a sin against God.

Sin and its consequences deserve serious attention. Where is the politician, the educator, the industrialist, the minister, the movement leader, the athlete, the celebrity who will pick up the torch?

A Right to Sin?

I listened to a Christian woman who recently learned that her husband has been leading a double life in an affair for the last several years. This is a common story these days. When she found out, she was so irate she could have killed him. She turned to her old source of peace and comfort—a bottle of wine. She told herself she had a right to get drunk. (Drunkenness is also a sin.) Somehow, as she felt the soothing effects of the wine, she remembered that she had regressed. She had exchanged wine as a source of peace instead of looking to Jesus. She repented on the spot of the evil thoughts she had toward her husband and the other woman and asked the Lord to forgive her for allowing anger and hatred to rule her heart.

She still faces the problem, but she changed from a wildly furious woman intent on compounding her problem by getting drunk and alienating herself from God. Instead she is contemplating what to do in a spirit of goodwill toward a husband and a woman who have deceived her and made a mockery out of marriage vows.

Living together peacefully is a simple matter of living by the Spirit. Gratifying the sinful nature has spawned complex personal, marital, social, national, and international problems. Remember, however, that you are only a prayer away from originating the beginnings of a transformed life. God is standing by. You can run your finger down those lists of sins. If you identify a sin, it can be dealt with by turning Godward through His Son. If you confess your sin, He is faithful and just and will forgive you and purify you from all unrighteousness (see 1 John 1:9).

The Flesh vs. the Spirit

My wife and I were guests in a Mennonite home. Our hosts read us a refreshing devotional out of their church publication. It summarizes the battle of the flesh versus the Spirit:

> There are countless Christians fighting a battle that is already lost, trying in their own strength to overcome the subtleties of sin. That is a battle you can fight all your days, but I tell you now, you cannot win! It is a battle already lost, lost in the first Adam, who was made a living soul, and died; but the last Adam, Jesus Christ, has already defeated sin and death and hell, and Satan himself! Why not accept in Him the victory the He has already won? Victory over the flesh is not to be attained—it is to be received.

"Walk in the Spirit, and you shall not fulfill the lust of the flesh" (Gal. 5:16). No matter what it is that threatens you, if you walk in the Spirit, you can turn around and face your enemy. You can "take him by the tail" and find him helpless and harmlesss in your hands, for God has already bruised the serpent's head! (see Gen. 3:15; Heb. 2:14). In other words, to walk in the Spirit is to *assume* by faith the victory with which He credits you. God will vindicate your assumption and make it real in your experience.

Now the devil loves to invert truth and turn it into a lie, and probably what he has been saying to you is this: "*Try* not to fulfill the lusts of the flesh, and *then* you will walk in the Spirit," as though the latter were a reward for the former. He knows that in this way, he will keep you preoccupied with yourself, instead of being preoccupied with Christ.

Nothing is more nauseating or pathetic than the flesh trying to be holy! The flesh has a perverted bent for righteousness—but such righteousness as it may achieve is always self-righteousness; and self-conscious righteousness is always full of self-praise. This produces the extrovert, who must always be noticed, recognized, consulted, and applauded. On the other hand, when the flesh in pursuit of self-righteousness fails, instead of being filled with self-praise, it is filled with self-pity, and this produces the introvert. A professional "case" for professional counselors!

The devil does not care whether you are an extrovert or an introvert. He does not care whether you succeed or whether you fail in the energy of the flesh, or whether you are filled with self-pity or self-praise. He knows that in both cases you will be preoccupied with yourself, not with Christ. You will be egocentric rather than Deo-centric— self-centered rather than God-centered.

Satan will seek to persuade you that "walking in the Spirit" is simply the consequence of your pious endeavor not to fulfill the "lusts of the flesh." Of course he is the author of the lusts of the flesh. By subtly confusing the means for the end, he will rob you of what he knows to be your only possibility of victory.

Is that what you have been trying to do? You have been trying not to fulfill the lust of the flesh in order to walk in the Spirit. You are fighting a battle already lost. What God has said to you is this, "Walk in the Spirit" (in an attitude of total dependence upon Him, exposing everything to Him) "and you shall not fulfill the lust of the flesh." You will then be enjoying through Him the victory that Christ has already won. To walk in the Spirit is not a reward—it is the means! It is to enjoy the saving life of Christ!

As you take every step in an attitude of total dependence upon the Lord Jesus Christ who indwells you by His Spirit, He celebrates in you the victory. He has already won over sin and death and Satan.

◆

4

Methods of Counseling

It may sound corny to a non-Christian. It may make a person committed to the "scientific method" smile. It may make an atheist furious. But when a biblical counselor steps into the consulting room, he is Christ's ambassador, as though God were making His appeal through him. He proceeds by faith in God's Word.

> Trust in the LORD with all your heart, and lean not on your own understanding; in all your ways acknowledge Him, and He shall direct your paths.
>
> Prov. 3:5–6

The biblical counselor may have reviewed the source of his faith:

And my speech and my preaching were not with persuasive words of human wisdom, but in demonstration of the Spirit and of power.

1 Cor. 2:4

While writing this very chapter, the good Lord allowed Kerry Skinner and me a glimpse of His power. Following are a few stories that shows the power of God.

Case Study: Loss of a Daughter

A couple who were not members of the church where Kerry served came to him for help. Their twenty-two-month-old daughter, Katlyn, drowned in the family pool. Their four-year-old son, Troy, was developing behavior problems. Several times each day he asked why Katlyn died.

Kerry asked the parents, Keith and Lynn, why they came to see him. Keith said they needed help with the boy. They were Christians, so they came to the church.

Kerry then asked Lynn if there were any problems in their eight-year marriage. This question was like lancing a boil. In a torrent of impassioned words, she described a marriage that was troubled from the beginning and had escalated into an unbearable relationship since the drowning. She was furiously angry at Keith.

Kerry replied that Katlyn's death did not cause their problems; it revealed them. He told them that he knew they just lost their daughter but their needs were in their heart. If it were not Katlyn's death, it would have been something else that brought it to the forefront.

He showed them the chart (page 42) and asked them if anything stood out to them.

Keith said, "My psychologist calls these natural emotions, but I know they are really sin." The chart showed the couple in black and white that they had a sin problem.

Kerry gave them the workbook *The Heart of the Problem* and asked them to return in a week, provided they did the daily exercise in the workbook.

They arrived a week later in Kerry's office, shoulders up and relaxed. Clearly something good had happened during the week. They returned two more times but then were able to handle their problems between themselves and God. Lynn had made a 180-degree turn and Keith was talking to his wife again.

Eighteen Months Later

Kerry and I visited them eighteen months later. They were eager to tell us their story.

Keith: When we came the second time, Kerry asked with his usual laid-back, smiley manner how things were going.

Lynn: As soon as I started going through the book the first week and having that time with God every day, it showed me that what I was doing was nothing but rotten sin. It was wrong and I was not entitled to be angry and bitter.

Kerry: So the key all along was God?

Keith: Yes. I think another point that really helped the first week and why we improved so quickly was because we were talking and sharing with each other at night.

Dr. Brandt: Was *The Heart of the Problem* workbook the vehicle that enabled you to begin talking again?

Keith: Right. We would show each other what we wrote down. The question every day on the end of the page is "Who are you going to share this with?" I always named Lynn and she always named me, so at night before we went to bed we would read each other's book. We were seeing new insights of each other—things that we did not know about each other and that we were going through. She began to realize the deep pain I was experiencing. You tell

God more personal things than you tell anybody. I was sharing those things with God and with her. She was sharing back and we realized how much we were both in pain. All of the things we were confessing to God, He was removing. We were yielding that way.

Lynn: We told you that Troy was asking everyday why did Katlyn die and we didn't really know what to do for him. You said, "There is a problem in your heart, and, therefore, there is a problem in your home. You don't have peace in your home. When you have peace in your heart, there is peace in your home. Troy won't need any counseling. He will be fine." Even though I knew that there wasn't peace in my home, when you said that, it really made me see the whole picture. That is why he was insecure and having behavior problems. It was just like it opened up the whole thing that maybe there was hope. Maybe we could somehow get through it.

Keith: That was the second session. You asked us how Troy was doing, and we just looked at each other. We hadn't thought about it. Troy hasn't asked the question once, why did Katlyn die. It was a miracle—it happened the day after we started reading the book.

Kerry: All of a sudden Troy stopped having problems?

Keith: Yes.

Kerry: He received his peace because there was peace in the home.

Keith: Right.

Kerry: Isn't it amazing how God can do that?

Dr. Brandt: This has been consistent now?

Kerry: At least a year and a half.

Lynn: It will be two years in July that Katlyn died.

Keith: Something else I wanted to bring up too: Mine and Troy's relationship is now the one that I wanted. He's the son I always dreamed of. He and I have a real close bond with each other. The Lord healed that. On top of that, I worked through the bitterness and anger I had toward my mom and my father. As a matter of fact, I called my father and told him I forgave him for everything. I told him I loved him. We are still not talking on a regular basis, but I am at peace with that situation. God just threw that in for good measure. He worked that out for me and He worked the issues out with my mom. I could go on with stories about my past, but the point is, it doesn't matter. The Lord healed that.

Human Help but No Cure

Some background material will help to understand this story. Keith was in charge of development marketing for a thirty-million-dollar-a-year company. He loved his work, and his paycheck was more than enough to live in a large home. There was plenty of money for food, clothes, cars, travel, and entertaining. The company began cutting back on management people. Suddenly, Keith was out of a job. They spent all he made so he was broke. Lynn, pregnant, had to go to work as a physical therapist.

Keith would not consider a job that was not on the level of his last job. He had been out of work four months when the drowning occurred.

Lynn was very bitter. She never agreed with his lavish spending. She resented his refusal to seek out a lesser job. She worked and he stayed home with the children. The day Katlyn died, Keith was taking a nap. Troy, the four-year-old, woke his daddy up to tell him about Katlyn. He rushed to the pool and found her floating face-down.

Troy fluctuated between blaming himself and blaming his dad. Troy would tell Keith that he should have been awake. The boy was going through play therapy, but it did not help. Lynn was consumed with anger and resentment toward her husband, and he carried a heavy load of guilt.

They went to see Compassionate Friends, a support group. Each meeting was a "feeling guilty party." Next, they went to a SIDs (Sudden Infant Death Syndrome) group. That group disbanded. For the last two months all three were seeing a clinical psychologist.

Lynn felt guilty about having a baby to replace Katlyn. She resented working. She criticized everything Keith did. He didn't fight back because he felt so guilty.

One night she vented a load of anger at Keith. "You killed my daughter, you are overweight, you don't have a good relationship with my son, and you can't find a job!"

Keith wouldn't talk. Bringing it up made him feel more guilt. So he stopped talking.

Keith: I was working about twelve hours a day, six days a week, and working on weekends at home. My dream was to have a son and to have a close relationship. I grew up with a mom who had four marriages and I never had a father. My whole goal was that one day I would have a son and I was going to be the father that I never had. But now, Troy wouldn't kiss me goodnight or even talk to me. When I was home without work for the four months, my relationship with Katlyn and I grew. We were inseparable. We got real close and I became the Mr. Mom. Troy and I got to be a little closer, but still there was this resentment. When Katlyn drowned, our relationship got unbelievably worse. He hated me. He would not talk to me. So we went to a clinical psychologist. She validated everything. She was saying, "That's OK. It's normal to feel this way—to feel anger and bitterness and guilt."

Lynn: I don't think Keith really even had a clue what I was missing. His basic attitude was that he provided a home and a good income for us. I got to go shopping whenever I wanted to and spend money and have the kids dressed impeccably. He felt that was where his responsibility ended. He didn't see that I needed a little help with the kids or the house. He expected me to do all of that because his mom had done all of that. His mom had kept an immaculate house, but she had never sat down and read a book to him or his brother. I was more like my mom. I actually wanted to spend time with my kids rather than clean my house all the time and never sit down. I felt totally trapped. I couldn't leave because of God, number one. However, I loved my kids more than I loved God. I definitely loved my kids more than I loved my husband. My priorities were out of whack.

Kerry: So, it was God who kept you in the marriage?

Lynn: Yes.

Keith: Yes. We were seeing a psychologist, and I was also working through a lot of problems with my past. Because of my mom's four marriages, there was a lot of built-up anger and resentment toward my dad. I had not seen him since I was nine. My mom was an alcoholic. I had a lot of bitterness that I didn't realize. I never talked about anything negative. I was always positive. The psychologist wanted me to talk about all the negatives. She said that is part of the healing process. Every time I talked to her, I felt good for the time being, but I noticed after I left her, I started feeling a little guilty. It was a temporary relief but it wasn't a cure.

Dr. Brandt: How long did you see her?

Keith: Probably about two months.

Lynn: I was getting more and more resentful because I was getting more and more pregnant and I was bartering to keep our heads above water. Because we couldn't afford counseling, I was giving massages to this psychologist and her son, as well as the woman who was working with Troy in play therapy. I was coming toward the end of my pregnancy, so both of us would soon be out of work.

Keith: Troy was getting a lot more violent and angry. Counseling from the world really wasn't going anywhere but I felt like it was at least better than nothing. I was getting some relief from the pain. Lynn had a copy of the original textbook of Dr. Brandt's. She read a couple of chapters, and I asked her what she thought of it. She said it seemed to be pretty strong stuff. That's all she said. We had been praying, "Lord, we really need something more." We knew we weren't getting better.

When both of our counselors went on vacation, we had no one to go to. Kerry was the last choice.

Kerry: Many times when a person comes to the church, they have already exhausted every other avenue. Last resort, Kerry Skinner.

Lynn: Well, what really impressed me to go see him was that Lauren, a quiet person, wrote me a note and said, "Lynn, I really think that you need to go see this man at my church. I know this would help you. His office is already expecting your call." I felt that it was God. He was definitely guiding me and I couldn't say no. I guess I was at the point where I was feeling very frustrated and trapped. I knew I couldn't get a divorce because I felt there had been too much pain already. I couldn't do that to Troy. I felt that I disn't love my husband, or respect him. We were living in the same house but there was nothing, maybe friendship—maybe shared times. I had totally given up hope that we would ever have the kind of marriage that I had always wanted.

Keith: Lynn came to me and shared the letter from Lauren and I agreed to go.

Lynn: He had actually made statements about our marriage like, "I think our marriage should just be able to coast along on its own." I never could quite figure out what he was talking about, but his attitude was that you should just be OK. I thought, *You don't have a clue, do you?*

Keith: Well, I was trying.

Lynn: He really didn't understand. I would be in tears and say, "Keith can we get some counseling? Can we talk to somebody?"

Keith: One thing that spoke to me in the first week of *The Heart of the Problem* was about sin and why Christians were so unhappy. We tried to go to other sources to get relief, but God loves and knows us better than anybody. He has the perfect prescription for our lives if we just ask Him for it. I never thought of it that way. *Experiencing God* brought us closer to that personal relationship with God. But *The Heart of the Problem* helped us work through the details.

We looked through our notes and couldn't believe we're the same people. The workbook asks you to let God clean your heart over and over again. I thought that was good because you need to get in the habit of going before God daily and being cleansed.

The Holy Spirit's Role in Biblical Counseling

At first glance, many pastors would not want to touch the previous case. Kerry had very little information to go on. He did have the guidance of the Holy Spirit, who knows the heart. This story illustrates the power of God to anyone who will listen. Look at the chart on the next page and see what happens when the counselor, the counselee(s), and the Holy Spirit are in the room:

1. God has a purpose.

2. His Holy Spirit takes the Word of God and speaks to both the counselor and the counselee.

3. Truth is revealed to both the counselor and counselee.

4. The result of the Truth being revealed is a changed life for both the counselor and counselee.

5. Both counselor and counselee are to obey what was revealed to them and are to walk in a continuing relationship with God.

Back to the biblical counselor. He or she enters the consulting room mindful of a biblical caution: He who answers

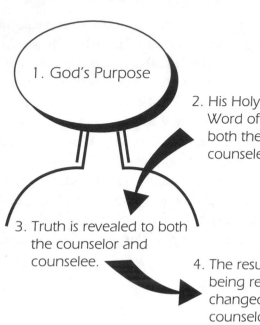

1. God's Purpose

2. His Holy Spirit takes the Word of God and speaks to both the counselor and the counselee.

3. Truth is revealed to both the counselor and counselee.

4. The result of the Truth being revealed is a changed life for both the counselor and counselee.

5. Both counselor and counselee are to obey what was revealed to them and are to walk in a continuing relationship with God.

a matter before he hears it, it is folly and shame to him" (Prov. 18:13).

Biblical counseling is a special kind of relationship. It is not a social call. You are listening for a biblical principle being violated. You may pick up on it in the first sentence. Continue listening until you get enough data to present your diagnosis based on their own data.

There is a fine line in listening to their story. You need to hear enough that they feel you understand the situation. Listen with compassion. People need to be heard. Help them bring out all the facts. But you don't need to be a garbage dump for things unnecessary to be expounded upon.

They cannot deny their sin if the biblical principle fits the data. This may take twenty minutes or three sessions. You hold the mirror of God's standard before them. Ask them what God is saying to them about this situation in the light of Scripture. This is self-confrontation. The goal is to bring them to the point of agreeing with the biblical principle.

At that point, you make the judgment call. Do they want spiritual help? If so, you can proceed. If not, you are stumped. If their problem is sin, the Good News is that Jesus died to save them from their sin and empower them to walk in the Spirit. And that is between them and God. You can not help them there.

Their happiness or misery is not based on their circumstances nor on the people in their lives, but on whatever spirit that controls them from within. The answer to their distress is the Spirit of God. Change will come when they repent of their sins and accept Christ as Savior as One who can give them His Spirit. Accepting Jesus as Lord and Savior does not take away their problems—He is the resource for dealing with them.

One does not need a degree in psychotherapy or need to be a professional licensed counselor in order to give biblical counsel to another. Often people will ask, "Who are you to give advice? Do you have a degree in counseling?" I wonder how many people there are who have turned elsewhere for help because Christians felt unqualified to share their knowledge of God. As a result, how many marriages have ended in divorce, how many lives have ended in suicide, or how many people are dependent on mood-altering drugs in order to see the light of another day?

As we examine the Word of God, we see that education alone is not what qualified the people of God to be used by God. For example, Noah did not have a degree in architecture nor did he have a background in zoology. Why would God choose Noah to build the ark and lead the people and animals to safety? Think about it. Noah did not even know what rain was. What then qualified Noah? The answer is found in Genesis 6:9: "Noah walked with God." Over the centuries, God has not changed. He delights in using His people to accomplish His work. God works through those who love Him, those who walk with Him as Noah did.

Following are some accounts of how God is using ordinary people to speak His truth. The Spirit of God takes the Word of God and pierces the heart of the individual and, as a result, lives are being radically changed.

Case Study: A Marriage Problem?

One evening some friends from the church called. Kathy and Michael had been struggling in their relationship with one another for quite some time. That evening they were desperate and asked for help. Kathy tells their story as follows:

> After I quit my job to stay home with the twins, a wall seemed to separate Michael and me. We were baffled. I felt guilty for leaving my job and placing the burden of all the finances on my husband. The financial burden, however, did not seem to bother Michael. The guilt lead to frustration and the frustration would always lead to verbal confrontation ending in an argument. We were unable to communicate and always at each other's throat. Something had to change; we could not go on like this.
>
> We then called our friends Kerry and Elaine and asked if they would talk with us. They prayed for us and Kerry began to share from God's Word concerning sin. He then handed us a piece of paper. On one side of this paper was listed the works of the flesh taken from several passages of

Scripture. On the other side was listed the fruit of the Spirit. We now call this piece of paper the "sin list," for that evening God revealed to Michael and me how much anger and resentment we had in our lives.

Kerry helped us to understand the meaning of true repentance. He then handed us a workbook, *The Heart of the Problem*. As Michael and I began to work in this book, our eyes began to open and we could see clearly that the heart of our problem was sin. This led to true repentance. Our relationship with God was restored, and the wall that separated my husband and me fell. Since this time, we have had the opportunity to share with person after person how God changed our lives.

Case Study: Hopeless

After Christmas, Elaine received a phone call from a single parent by the name of Debra. Debra's children had visited the church for Vacation Bible School. The oldest child had also attended our summer children's camp. A few days before Christmas, I began to think about Debra and wondered if she needed help with Christmas for her children. She did not share her needs with me, so I ended the conversation by saying, "Debra, if you ever need anything, please call me."

About three weeks later Debra called. Her voice sounded very anxious and desperate. "Can you help me? They want to hospitalize me for depression and I don't want to go. They won't let me go home unless I receive some counseling immediately. I couldn't think of anyone else to call. They keep giving me anti-depressants and I just can't take them. Oh, please say you can help me."

Before we were through speaking the nurse practitioner picked up the phone. She began checking out my counseling qualifications. She asked if my husband or I were qualified to counsel people who are depressed. My answer to her questions was, "I've spoken with many ladies who have suffered from depression. I don't claim to be a 'professional counselor.' I am, however, a biblical counselor and will be glad to spend some time with Debra."

I called a friend who had just gone through such a struggle, and together we went to visit Debra. My friend shared her personal testimony of how God had revealed to her the source of her depression was anger. The first step I took was to find out if Debra was a Christian. She shared with us about her salvation experience and seemed to be very secure in that decision. I then began to show her from God's Word the difference between sin-controlled living and Spirit-controlled living. I then gave Debra a "sin" list found in *The Heart of the Problem*. On this was listed from scripture sins of the mind, emotions, mouth, and behavior. We prayed and asked God to point out to Debra anything He saw in her heart.

> And there is no creature hidden from His sight, but all things are naked and open to the eyes of Him to whom we must give account.
>
> Heb. 4:13

After prayer, Debra looked at this list. I will never forget her words. "Has anyone ever checked everything on this list?"

God had opened her eyes to see the sin that was separating her from Him and, as a result, sending her into depression. Drugs, alcohol, sex, none of these things that she had turned to for help from depression was working. After we left, Debra confessed her sins one at a time to God and repented. She asked God to cleanse her and fill her with His Spirit, which is love, joy, peace, gentleness, goodness, faith, meekness, and temperance. That night Debra slept like a baby for the first time in many months.

There has been a radical change in her life, and all the glory goes to God.

Debra went back to her doctor and his comment was, "What happened to you, a miracle or something?"

She replied, "Yes, and I don't need all of this medicine you keep giving me. What I needed was the Lord in my life." Debra is surrounded daily by people who are struggling with the same problems that she had. She is now sharing with these people what she has learned through reading daily from the Bible and *The Heart of the Problem*. Her latest comment to one of her friends who made mention of how peaceful and happy she appeared to be was, "You won't find this kind of peace and happiness in a bar. You will only find it in the Lord."

Opposite Approaches

Catharsis

The servant of the Lord needs to understand an old familiar term—catharsis. *Ventilating* is a similar word. It means giving a counselee the opportunity to express their thoughts, feelings, and emotions—assisting them to clarify the same. The counselee is assured of a sympathetic, non-judgmental, loving ear. The expression inevitably involves describing unreasonable demands, lack of being loved and understood, ignored needs, neglect, cruelty, conflict, criticism, physical or sexual abuse. The response of the counselee to such treatment is anger, bitterness, resentment, hatred, malice, ill will, deception, rebellion.

If the counselee has been reading secular literature or has received secular counseling, then the counselee would assume that the response to the treatment received is the result of the treatment. In fact, a rapidly growing number of Christians, even pastors, would agree with the secular conclusion: The counselee is a victim of the past.

To lend a loving, sympathetic ear that enables a person to get these things "off the chest" is a source of great satisfaction to the counselor. The benefit to the counselee is great, blessed relief. It is as much a relief as a drug that deadens unbearable pain. But it is relief, not healing.

Carl Rogers popularized nondirective counseling. You gently and lovingly help your counselee verbalize whatever is on their mind. The objective is to help the counselee clarify conflicts, thoughts, emotions, goals without influencing the process. This is very helpful, resulting in precious relief of tension.

These words spoken by Jesus seem to support non-judgmental thinking:

> "Judge not, that you be not judged. For with what judgment you judge, you will be judged; and with the same measure you use, it will be measured back to you."
>
> Matt. 7:1–2

This verse is often interpreted to mean that judging means unloving disapproval. I understand this verse to mean the person making judgments is abiding by the same guidelines that they are using to evaluate the counselee's choices.

In biblical counseling, you must be clear about your objective. Your counselee should understand that this is a specialized kind of listening. You are listening to help the counselee decide whether choices made comply or deviate from biblical principles. You must have the approval of the counselee in order to do this. This process involves making judgments. Your counselee may resist the process even though it was agreed upon. You make judgments momentarily as you go along, comparing the story to biblical principles. There is no one to consult with. On what basis do you make such decisions?

If any of you lack wisdom, let him ask of God, who gives to all liberally and without reproach, and it will be given to him. But let him ask in faith, with no doubting, for he who doubts is like a wave of the sea driven and tossed by the wind.

James 1:5–6

If you lack wisdom, you go into the presence of God and by faith believe that He is guiding you. The promise is,

Be anxious for nothing, but in everything by prayer and supplication, with thanksgiving, let your requests be made known to God; and the peace of God, which surpasses all understanding, will guard your hearts and minds through Christ Jesus.

Phil. 4:6–7

If you find yourself under such pressure with this great responsibility that you worry and cannot sleep at nights, there is something wrong with your approach. God will keep your heart and mind if you are rightly related to Him. If you do anything for a counselee, it is to communicate your confidence in God and His Word, the Bible, to that person.

At this point we come to a watershed that divides the nonbiblical counselor from the biblical counselor. Both of them will inevitably deal with responses to life such as anger, bitterness, resentment, sexual immorality, malice, ill will, rebellion, deception, and the like. If so, then the response of the counselee to the past is the result of a sinful heart. That is the greatest news a struggling counselee could receive. *It is only sin.* No need to struggle with the environment any more to find relief. Now they deal only with God. He will cleanse their heart from sin and fill it with the Spirit. The humanist calls these *normal* human emotions and thinks we have the ability to manage them.

Facing the Problem

We must be careful not to consider relief from catharsis and the cleansing from sin as interchangeable. In fact, the counselee may only want the relief without the cleansing. Revealing what is in a sinful heart to a Christian counselor without repentance is like disrobing physically and then wishing they had kept their clothes on.

The counselor should be reluctant to allow catharsis to go very far without clarifying whether the person is asking for relief or the fullness of the Spirit.

So, there is the matter of making a judgment. What kind of relationship is this? Is it catharsis? If it is catharsis, the counselor would let somebody come and repeat the same thing maybe twice, maybe three times. This is a judgmental matter. They are talking about the same problem for the third time and have come to the place where the counselor must ask if this person is willing to think with him in terms of a resolution of this problem or not? "Do you see what we are doing? We are going round and round about the same problem. There is no point in that. If you are not prepared to go on, OK, but this is where we stop. You are wasting time and money."

Many counselees will not like it when you tell them that they are not facing their problems. They may not agree. "It is not my fault. It is my partner's fault. If my partner would change, everything would be all right." They will attempt to talk you out of it. They get mad; they pout; they cry. They stomp out of your office, but they do not change your mind.

You cannot speed up the process. You can only go as fast as they can go. You have a limited amount of time and it is important that you do not waste it. Do not spend time on useless information. When someone tells you something that they have already told you, remind them that they have already told you that.

If you are in the business of smoothing over unhealthy relationships, then you will listen to whatever they choose to talk about. But if you are interested in helping people, then you must be willing to see people disturbed. You cannot get away from that. You must be firm at times. Counseling means dealing with troubled people. That means you will be face to face with hostile, jealous, stubborn, resentful, bitter, envious, explosive, delicate, tender situations. Counseling implies all of this. Your spirit is important.

You may be as kind and loving as you can possibly be. That does not mean that you will get that kind of a response from the counselee. They are the ones who need counseling. You are the one who ought to be the anchor in the rock. You are the one who should be steady and consistent. You do not need to be defensive.

Ways to Be a More Effective Counselor

The Counselor's Heart

When people are down on you, be sure your heart is right toward them. Do they like you is not the question. Is your heart right toward them? This is the important question. You must continuously evaluate what kind of a relationship this is. Is it catharsis, or comparison with biblical principles? The relationship can change from one to another.

I would rather have a man walk out of my office twice as troubled as when he walked in if the truth produces such a result. If a physician wanted you to feel comfortable when you walked out of his office, he would not treat you like he would if he wanted to cure you. What are you interested in doing? This is a time to examine your goals.

Our objective is to work ourselves out of a job with that particular person. Your own personality comes into play. Some counselors may not feel comfortable unless they have a half dozen people leaning on them because of their own needs. Their own source of peace and strength is not in God, but in the fact that they have certain people who get starry-eyed when they walk past. They worship the counselor. You ought to be careful about that. Praise is as hard to handle as criticism. To some counselees who adore you, the next time they come you must tell them something they do not want to hear. If their adoration is more important to you than their adjustment, then what you say will be colored by your own needs. Does that make sense? Then be careful about that. You are always looking for something to realistically praise, but do not be afraid of pointing out a weakness. We are just human enough and needy enough that we tend to get out of balance either on one side or the other. For this reason, we need each other.

Self-Evaluation

One reason for recording a speech or an interview is to review it yourself. I listen to some of my tapes with a red face. It is a big help to be reassured that we are doing the right thing in the right way with the right attitude. It would not hurt you to let your assistant sit in your office for a day and just watch you. Can you take it? It is not very easy, I can tell you that. I am convinced that to be most effective you must be able to stand the scrutiny of other people. I think this is one of the weaknesses among Christians. We tremble at evaluation. What are we afraid of?

If you are saying the right thing and doing the right thing, you will not worry about who observes you. If you are saying the right thing, you do not need to remember what you said. We keep ourselves away from a lot of pressure by doing the right thing.

You would be wise to confer regularly among staff who teach, preach, or counsel, with evaluation in mind. If you are operating in your little cubicle and you do not think it is anybody else's business what you do, you are apt to get yourself in a lot of trouble. You had better be sure that you keep the channel of communication open and let key people know what is going on in a particular case.

> "Only take heed to yourself, and diligently keep yourself, lest you forget the things your eyes have seen, and lest they depart from your heart all the days of your life. And teach them to your children and your grandchildren."
>
> Deut. 4:9

Keep your soul diligently. If you are angry, you are dealing with your own sins. You are the architect of your own misery. This is on a daily basis. Take care of your own frustrations, resentment, anger, pride. Our tendency is to look the other way. Acknowledge these things to the Lord. We tend to blame others or circumstances.

The important fact about biblical counseling is dealing with a man's spirit. If you are frustrated over someone being late, it reveals your spirit. First, saturate your heart with the Word of God. You must have some assurance of being able to practice it. Then when you fall on your face, you can pick yourself up and know how to restore your soul.

First Disciples, Then Counselors

Question: I take it from what you have said thus far, we should become disciples first before we can become counselors, correct?

Answer: I am a follower of the Master. Anyone who approaches me, needs to know right off the bat that I am a Christian. I love the Bible. I have found life in Christ—I am happy, content, my record proves it. It is as Jesus Christ said,

"I have come that they may have life, . . . more abundantly."

John 10:10

I have found the abundant life and can help you find it. But it involves following after Jesus Christ, the Master.

How far can you take people? As far as you have come. You can only teach them what you know. It is an expanding knowledge of the Word that gives you an expanding ministry. If you do not want that Bible "stuff," that's all I have to offer. Follow after me through the Bible, and you will find that the God of Peace will be with you as He is with me. I am growing up and improving (like tennis). The more you play and improve your strokes, the better you play. But, if you keep on doing the wrong thing over and over, you get worse. If you follow what you have learned about our Lord, you will find yourself steadily improving.

> The LORD is my strength and my shield; my heart trusted in Him, and I am helped; therefore my heart greatly rejoices, and with my song I will praise Him.
>
> Ps. 28:7

Basic Principle: If joy is not happening, then something is wrong. You *can* enjoy a trial.

> You will keep him in perfect peace, whose mind is stayed on You.
>
> Isa. 26:3

> Great peace have those who love Your law, and nothing causes them to stumble.
>
> Ps. 119:165

> The work of righteousness will be peace, and the effect of righteousness, quietness and assurance forever.
>
> Isa. 32:17

The effect of righteousness is quietness. If you have lost your peace, you need to find out what you are doing wrong. This depends on your comparing your life with knowledge of the Bible. We need to be disciples of the Master, and if we are, we study, study, study, what He wants us to know. That means a working knowledge of the Bible taken seriously.

Counseling and the Body of Christ

Question: How does a Christian and biblical counseling relate to the total body of Christ?

Answer: When I started counseling, I would see a counselee one hour and then again the next week. What the counselee did in between was up to him or her. I have come to realize this is not the best way to deal with people. The way to be sustained as an individual is to have fellowship with fellow believers and to be reminded of the Word of God. The simplest and finest and best way to do that is to be exposed to the Word of God on a weekly basis.

If I am really going to help people, there are certain things I must expect of them. I must recommend some Bible-believing churches. I want them to work hard to get some help (i.e., go to church Sunday morning and night, Sunday School Class, get acquainted with Christian people). I am a great believer in the ministry of the Church. People need to find themselves a church that warms their heart on a weekly basis. People will go for therapy for a year and still not be helped. But what would happen to people who expose themselves to a good church for a year?

I expect people, if at all possible, to have previous exposure to me before I see them personally, such as:

1. Attend some public meetings
2. Read my books
3. Listen to some audio tapes
4. View some video tapes

If people do what this material says, they may not need to see me. If they do not like what they read or hear, there is no point in seeing me. The only reason for seeing me, then, would be for clarification, not argumentation.

"If you abide in My word, you are My disciples indeed. And you shall know the truth, and the truth shall make you free."

John 8:31–32

The Biblical Standard

Question: Could you comment on some of the do's and don't of biblical counseling?

Answer: Think biblical. When you listen to someone, you are listening for deviation from the Word as a standard. Your effectiveness will depend on your knowledge and application of the Bible. So it is the Word you need. Leave secular study aside until you are knowledgeable in the Word. These Bible verses support biblical counseling:

Blessed are the undefiled in the way, who walk in the law of the Lord! Blessed are those who keep His testimonies, who seek Him with the whole heart! They also do no iniquity; they walk in His ways. You have commanded us to keep Your precepts diligently. Oh, that my ways were directed to keep Your statutes! Then I would not be ashamed, when I look into all your commandments. I will praise You with uprightness of heart, when I learn Your righteous judgments. I will keep Your statutes; oh, do not forsake me utterly. How can a young man cleanse his way? By taking heed according to Your word. With my whole heart I have sought You; Oh, let me not wander from Your commandments! Your word I have hidden in my heart, that I might not sin against You. Blessed are You, O Lord! Teach me Your statutes. With my lips I have declared all the judgments of Your mouth. I have rejoiced in the way of Your testimonies, as much as in all riches. I will meditate on your precepts, and contemplate Your ways. I will delight myself in Your statutes; I will not forget Your word.

Ps. 119:1–16

If you take this psalm seriously, you will see the importance of having a working knowledge of the Bible in your head because you have Christ, the Truth, in your heart.

◆

5

Counseling Distinctives

Day by day the pastor and the biblical counselor are privileged to minister to people. We see very clearly that it is the spirit within a man that causes him to rejoice or to despair.

Dealing with the human spirit is the distinctive mark and the basis of blessing to thousands of persons. Such a guiding principle did not spring from textbooks or blossom overnight. The beginnings go back sixty years.

Dr. Brandt's Testimony

In those days I attended a church that seemed solid and able to last forever. But I watched that church split over an issue. Persons whom I respected reacted in many different ways to a single set of facts.

I was a teenager. I rebelled against my church and family. For several years I lived directly opposite to what I was taught. Yet, within the same family, my sister was quite content. Eventually, I returned to the fold to accept the very persons and standards of conduct that I thought caused me so much distress.

My change was due to repenting of my sins and accepting Christ as my Savior—One who would give me His Spirit.

Later, I worked with men who would tell me their troubles. I heard many stories that repeated the pattern of my own experiences—that in a particular circumstance some people will be happy, but others will be greatly disturbed.

It became plain to me that human happiness or misery is not based on our circumstances or the people in our lives, but on which spirit controls us from within.

Certain of this, I returned to school to study psychology and related subjects. Eight years of study, observation, and guided experience only deepened my conviction that the answer to human distress is the Spirit of God. The fruit of the Spirit, Paul wrote in Galatians 5, is love, joy, peace, patience, kindness, goodness, faithfulness, gentleness, and self-control: against such there is no law. The logical conclusion, then, is a biblical approach to counseling.

Biblical Counseling and Secular Counseling

Similarities

How is biblical counseling like other counseling? In these ways:

- The counselor recognizes the distress of his counselee as evidence that a problem exists.

- The counselor helps the counselee tell the whole story, bringing out all the facts, pleasant or unpleasant.

- The counselor listens with compassion, accepting the counselee regardless of the story.

- The counselor treats the information with utmost care.

- The counselor grants the counselee the right to make his own decisions and to lead his own kind of life.

There are several instances when the approach of a biblical counselor and a humanist would be the same. Personnel selection is an example. The counselor must make a judgment on how the applicant will respond to the demands of a position. He studies the application form, autobiography, school transcripts, references, tests, work history, financial statement, and interview. Based on this data, the skilled counselor can produce a reasonably accurate description of how the applicant does and will respond to his environment.

The humanist and the biblical counselor can work side by side to this point, then we come to a fork in the road.

Differences

How does biblical counseling differ from secular counseling? In these ways:

- The biblical counselor compares his counselee's account with a fixed standard, the Bible.

All Scripture is given by inspiration of God, and is profitable for doctrine, for reproof, for correction, for instruction in righteousness, that the man of God may be complete, thoroughly equipped for every good work.

2 Tim. 3:16

- The biblical counselor points out to the counselee the areas in which his experience agrees or differs with the standard of life that God sets forth in Scripture. Whether the counselee will seek God's Spirit toward the people and circumstances in his life is the counselee's own decision. Bringing the counselee to this point is the distinctive of biblical counseling.

• The humanist seeks to determine how the environment has affected the applicant's responses to life, whereas the biblical counselor seeks to determine if the applicant lives by the Spirit or by the desires of the sinful nature.

This book focuses on the counselee's inner life. This is a specialized activity. It should be clear to the counselee that the goal of a counseling session is to discover how the counselee's story fits with biblical principles.

The Counselor's Intentions on Behalf of the Counselee

As a biblical counselor, you assume that counselees come to see you because they are reacting to their circumstances in an unacceptable manner. Your goal is to listen long enough so that a biblical principle being violated comes to *your* mind. Continue to listen until the data confirms your judgment and the counselee agrees (e.g., You both agree that he is a very angry man and hates his wife). This could take a half hour or three sessions.

Counselee Readiness

You must estimate when the counselee is ready to consider a biblical description of the problem and take some action. Then, you present your insight and leave the result with God. You will not fear being wrong when you are using the Bible as a mirror.

Your counselee has been telling you how angry his wife makes him. He has believed this for years. Now you are telling him that his anger is a work of the sinful nature. He needs a change of heart. He is instantly furious at you. You quietly tell him to think about it and see you next week.

I have found that the counselee's reactions (inner response) to the details cause the suffering. This is true regardless of the details of a life history—family background, interpersonal relations, environmental pressures, successes, failures, rejection, death, or whatever. The counselee is not walking in the Spirit, and as a result he is not thinking straight.

Usually there is a period of resistance. The counselee insists that the suffering is caused externally rather than internally. Kind, firm pressure from the counselor is needed to get acceptance of the internal problem. Once the counselee is firmly established Godward, I find that I am not needed in dealing with external problems.

I have learned that sincere seekers of help may initially resist a glimpse of their sinful selves. But if the glimpse has a ring of truth to it, they will have a second response. When they take another look, they must admit the truth. I have learned to look for that second reaction. Then we can move on.

> He who covers his sins will not prosper, but whoever confesses and forsakes them will have mercy.
>
> Prov. 28:13

Respect the devastating consequences of sin. Covering up your sin, instead of being freed from, is a roadblock to making behavior match the heart's desire.

> When I kept silent, my bones grew old through my groaning all the day long. For day and night Your hand was heavy upon me; my vitality was turned into the drought of summer. I acknowledged my sin to You, and my iniquity I have

not hidden. I said, "I will confess my transgressions to the Lord," and You forgave the iniquity [guilt] of my sin.

Ps. 32:3–5

People naturally rehearse their past as an explanation for present lack of peace and joy. They tend to explain their tensions by focusing on what someone else said or did. Or they may focus on some event—an accident, death, dirty trick, life, bad break, a loss, or a crisis.

People tend to resist when asked to recall problems and reactions they have not mentioned. They can readily recall their own sins but then disregard or dismiss or deny them. Discussing one's sins is usually disturbing to the counselee.

"Why did you do it?" is not a helpful question. It only helps the person to think up reasons they have not thought of before. The heart is deceitful. The person can persuade himself that his explanations are valid.

Almost everyone is capable of defining their problems and solving them with God's help. My first choice is to encourage a person to think of counseling as a last resort. If they can pray and absorb information and want to correct their ways with God's help, most people will find a way. God working through His Word, His church, good tapes, videos, books, and seminars offer all the help most people need.

"I Do Not Need Your Book"

A man came for help with an unmanageable teenager. I learned that he had a successful manufacturing and distribution business, but he hardly knew his child.

I asked him, "What would your business be like if you ran it like you do your family?"

"A shambles," he said.

I offered him my book on the family.

He solemnly replied, "I do not need your book. I know what to do." How true. He went home and did it. God knew his family better than I did. He simply needed to repent and return to God. God then could direct him in any way needed for the health of his family.

How will you approach the counselee? You must come to terms with the current wave of "scientific insights." From out of nowhere, it seems, the discovery has been made that restless, stressful people are victims of serious abuse in a murky past. It may be verbal, neglect, physical, or sexual. A specialized technique has been developed to dig out this past treatment. Therapists are requesting that children confront their parents with their new insights, and the parents are expected to accept responsibility for the child's present condition. The implication is that a victim is separated from God until fully aware of the past treatment. It seems that a public announcement is required as part of the therapy.

What light can God shed on our paths. What are we to do with unconscious material?

Unconscious Conflicts vs. Personal Responsibility

One thing I do, forgetting those things which are behind and reaching forward to those things which are ahead, I press toward the goal for the prize of the upward call of God in Christ Jesus. Therefore let us, as many as are mature, have this mind; and if in anything you think otherwise, God will reveal even this to you. Nevertheless, to the degree that we have already attained, let us walk by the same rule, let us be of the same mind.

Phil. 3:15–16

The Bible uses many words that indicate the ability of the counselee to consciously define problems and take action:

- come
- draw nigh
- search
- repent
- put off
- put on
- yield
- take

- commit
- believe
- receive
- confess
- let
- rest
- add
- remain

Notice the following verses:

For God so loved the world that He gave His only begotten Son, that whoever believes in Him should not perish but have everlasting life.

John 3:16

But as many as received Him, to them He gave the right to become children of God, to those who believe in His name.

John 1:12

"Come to Me, all you who labor and are heavy laden, and I will give you rest. Take My yoke upon you and learn from Me, for I am gentle and lowly in heart, and you will find rest for your souls."

Matt. 11:28–30

"Abide in Me, and I in you. As the branch cannot bear fruit of itself, unless it abides in the vine, neither can, unless you abide in Me."

John 15:4

Let all bitterness, wrath, anger, clamor, and evil speaking be put away from you, with all malice.

Eph. 4:31

Therefore, to him who knows to do good and does not do it, to him it is sin.

James 4:17

THE WORD FOR THE WISE

> No temptation has overtaken you except such as is common to man; but God is faithful, who will not allow you to be tempted beyond what you are able, but with the temptation will also make the way of escape, that you may be able to bear it.
>
> 1 Cor. 10:13

God's invitation is to believe, receive, abide, come, take. Frequently, an individual will protest that he has no willpower, that he is weak, that his case is special. He pleads for understanding, implying that if he were understood, he would be accepted as he is.

Of course it is true that all men are weak, unrighteous, sinful. It is also true that a disturbed individual needs to be understood.

Problem Analysis vs. Problem Resolution

But understanding a person and his problems does not change him. It only makes his need clear. He needs someone to reassure, instruct, and guide him to Christ who can change his heart. This change will not take place so long as the individual excuses himself by talking about the past or by blaming other people. His heart will be changed only when he repents of his sins, including his sinful reactions to others who may have mistreated him.

The Bible stresses individual ability to recognize and confess sin, to repent, and thus receive forgiveness, cleansing, and power.

The biblical counselor must recognize and deal with the inner nature of man—his mental, emotional and spiritual condition. Many pastors have been taught that psychological or emotional problems are out of their area of ministry—beyond their ability to handle. They feel that these problems are deeply buried in the counselee's past life and require a clinically trained person to ferret them out.

So-called clinical training does not involve God. It involves using the things of this world to find relief.

The words *psychology* and *emotional* do not appear in the Bible. The acts of the sinful nature and the fruit of the Spirit are the terms used in the Bible. If the acts of the sinful nature are the problem, the person must look to God for help. If the person rejects appealing to God for help, the biblical counselor has nothing else to offer.

It is important to note that acts of the sinful nature are not beyond God's ability to heal. It is incorrect to say that these acts are beyond the pastor's or the biblical counselor's level of competency. It is correct to say that the person has rejected turning to God, and has chosen to live with the sinful nature.

My own experience with disturbed people has revealed that most of them have a similar background. They have been mistreated, misunderstood, hated, rejected, and subjected to great external pressures. And these people have responded to such treatment with bitterness, resentment, anger, stubbornness, rebellion, jealousy, and an unforgiving spirit. Obviously one cannot change his past. His maltreatment by other people may be beyond his control. But this does not explain his bitterness, jealousy, etc. He is fully responsible for these emotional responses, which God calls the acts of the sinful nature.

When anyone turns to God, He will forgive and will change our responses to people and events in the future.

Your Method of Counseling

At the 1966 World Congress on Evangelism in Berlin, Halverson commented on methodology in evangelism:

Andrew's approach was different from Peter's and both men in turn were unlike Paul, this one who determined to be "all things to all men, that he might save some." Neither Peter nor Paul laid down systems or methods, except in the most general sense, whereby their disciples might propagate the Gospel. They were to transmit it to still others; just how this message would be propagated was left to the personality and gifts of each messenger ("Personal Evangelism," *Decision*, V2I:11, Jan. 1967).

This same principle applies to counseling. Dealing with individuals and their needs is more a matter of getting across a message than following a single established method. Each pastor will follow his own distinctive way and use his own choice of words. But even so, the following basic factors are essential in effective counseling:

Factor 1: Be Compassionate

To be an effective counselor, you must be a loving, compassionate person. You must love the counselee enough to present him with God's truth regardless of what the truth may suggest for him. When the rich young ruler came to Jesus and asked what he must do to inherit eternal life, "Jesus, looking at him, loved him" (Mark 10:21).

But you must not force God's solution on the counselee. Remember that he has the freedom of choice. He can reject or accept God's answer to his problems. The rich young ruler "was sad at this word, and went away sorrowful, for he had great possessions" (Mark 10:22).

Factor 2: Listen to the Problem

If you are a compassionate pastor, you will want to listen carefully to the problem presented by the counselee. As a "specialist" in spiritual problems (problems of the spirit, the inner man), you will seek to discover the individual's attitudes and reactions toward people and circumstances. This may take three or four interviews. The process cannot be hurried.

You need not probe endlessly into the counselee's past. No one can change what has gone before. Counselor and counselee should be concerned with the counselee's current behavior and attitude, which reflect the past. As counselor, you will listen for evidences of carnality—acts of the sinful nature. Do not hesitate to do this, for you know that the blood of Jesus Christ can wash away sin and that the fruit of the Spirit can replace the acts of the sinful nature. You should have the same confidence in the benefits of God's message as the surgeon has in the benefits of an operation.

Listening is an art. Therefore, seek to improve your asking and listening skills. Read literature on techniques of listening and interviewing. Then as you gain experience in counseling, your interviewing ability will improve. Obviously, your one-hundredth counseling interview will go smoother than your first.

Factor 3: Point the Counselee to a Solution

Be sure you correctly understand the person's situation and his attitudes and reactions toward it. Do not jump to a solution hurriedly before you are sure of the exact nature of the problem. Many people will talk first about a "surface problem," which is not their real problem at all.

When you and the counselee agree on his real problem and understand his attitudes and reactions, you can then use the Bible as a mirror so the individual can see himself reflected there. At this point you need to be firm, but not stern. You need not strive with people, but faithfully, gently, patiently, and lovingly declare the Word of God. After all, doesn't the Bible give God's answers to people's basic problems and needs?

Some counselors do not feel they should suggest any solutions to their counselee's problems. They believe that the counselee must struggle and grope till he finally finds and accepts his own solution. But is it not true that the counselee has come to you because he wants help—not only in understanding his problem but in finding a solution to it? Why should you withhold God's answers to a person's problems when you know the answers? You should present God's solution from the Bible—and then it is up to the counselee to accept it or reject it.

If the individual is not a Christian, this is the time to present the plan of salvation—God's offer of forgiveness of sin through faith in Christ as one's personal Savior. If the individual is a Christian, this is the time to teach him that he is not walking in the Spirit. It is surprising how often Christians will gradually drift away from the Lord and accept their carnal emotional condition as "normal."

The next step is up to the counselee. He may repent, or he may not. He may want to go away and think about it. Or he may go away quite upset. Or he may ask to return for more help on clarifying the problem and understanding its solution.

Factor 4: Use Other Counseling Tools

At this point the pastor has some other tools to use in helping the person ponder the truth about himself. He can introduce the individual to a group in the body of Christ.

A trend in the counseling field today is the use of group therapy as a supplement to the counselor's personal contact with his or her counselee. It is believed there are insights to be gained by the counselee as he listens to the views of other people in his group that cannot be gained as readily by interacting with the counselor only. In a number of experiments today, selected lay people are being used to do counseling and group therapy.

This trend should be of great interest to you as a pastor. You should take a new look at the "spiritually therapeutic" value of the total church body life. It is true that the pastor's study has been and is a hallowed place for counseling many individuals and couples. But the pastor has other tools—the pulpit, prayer groups, Sunday School classes, youth groups, men's and women's groups, worship services, Bible studies, retreats.

In group work, many pastors have been doing for years (called Sunday School) what the secular counseling field is just beginning to do. Secular counselors are now beginning to realize that interaction with a group in addition to personal interviews is often more helpful to the counselee than contact with the counselor only.

The entire church body and small groups within it can help individuals judge the wisdom of their choices and attitudes. These contacts give individuals a point of reference from which to judge themselves.

Most of my counselees come as a result of my public speaking in churches. This is evidence that people respond to messages from the pulpit, Sunday School lessons, group Bible studies, weekend or week-long retreats. Messages and group contacts help many people bring their views and problems into focus. Then when they come to their pastor's study, they already have some concept of their problems and solutions. Therefore, after a person comes to you for individual counsel, seek to guide him into the life of other Christians in the church.

As a pastor you should be a specialist in helping people discern the thoughts and intents of the heart. Your basic tool is the Scriptures, which accurately mirror the soul. You have the happy task of showing disturbed people the way to the peace of God, which surpasses all understanding, will guard your hearts and minds through Christ Jesus.

Phil. 4:7

The counselor in private practice should be aware of such churches in his area.

Ten Procedural Tips

1. The counselor tends to be self-centered:
    * What does counselee think of me?
    * Am I leaving a good impression?
    * What will counselee tell others about me?

2. The counselee is likely to be preoccupied with one problem:
    * I'm scared ever since my accident.
    * I do not trust him since the affair.
    * I feel guilty since having premarital relations.
    * I could never please my father.
    * I'm always bitter toward my mother.

3. The counselor should listen for patterns:
    * history of temper tantrums
    * pattern of self-centeredness
    * evidence of stubbornness, pouting
    * history of irresponsibility

4. The counselor should listen for causes, not symptoms. Reactions are:
    * personal, not situational
    * personal, not circumstantial
    * personal, not interpersonal

5. Identify deeds of the sinful nature when you deal with resistance. People often use these words to avoid recognizing the deeds of the sinful nature:

- lost my head
- upset
- went to pieces
- crushed
- blew up
- deflated
- fed up
- tense
- lost control
- agitated

- under pressure
- depressed
- collapsed
- inferior
- broke down
- threatened
- torn up inside
- brokenhearted
- climbing a wall
- uptight

6. Look for these types of behaviors in your counselee:

- withdrawal
- defiance
- tears
- justification

- tantrums
- attack
- pouting
- illness

7. Learn to depend on your counselee's second reaction:

- When calmed down, the counselee realizes your diagnosis has a ring of truth to it.
- May not agree in spite of evidence.
- May not repent in spite of evidence.

He who disdains instruction despises his own soul, but he who heeds rebuke gets understanding.

Prov. 15:32

8. Lead your counselee to (or back to) proper fellowship with God:

- promise verses— giving hope

- strengthening

- confession
- repentance
- forgiveness
- growing
- homework

9. You should encourage:
   - involvement in a healthy church
   - reading Bible and biblically-based literature
   - listening to biblically based cassettes
   - developing a personal walk with God using resources such as *Experiencing God: Knowing and Doing the Will of God, The Heart of the Problem,* and *The Mind of Christ*
   - defining and solving personal, interpersonal, and environmental problems without your help.

10. You should assign:
    - Bible study
    - reading
    - cassettes

Summary

1. Avoid cold contacts.
2. Stress personal responsibility.
3. Up to 80 percent of counselees will reject help.
4. Do not promise to keep confidence. The counselee must trust your judgment. At times your knowledge of the counselee would jeopardize a life if you kept a confidence. The counselee may be stealing, unfaithful, suicidal, close to violence, or on drugs.
5. Always offer hope.

Now may the God of hope fill you with all joy and peace in believing, that you may abound in hope by the power of the Holy Spirit.

Rom. 15:13

Strengthened with all might, according to His glorious power, for all patience and longsuffering with joy.

Col. 1:11

6. Imparting knowledge does not always result in change.

7. Judge your success in counseling on accuracy and the Spirit of your presentation of biblical principles, not on the counselee's response.

Struggling toward the Truth

I was in a foreign country. A lady asked for help with many confusing thoughts.

She lived in a huge home that was carefully guarded. No one had ever tried to forceably enter. But because her husband was away on business most of the time, she agonized with a persistent fear of someone breaking in and harming her.

I proposed that she consider this verse:

There is no fear in love; but perfect love casts out fear.

1 John 4:18

I asked her, "Could it be that you resent being left along in a foreign country?" I requested that she write down her response to my suggestion and attend a public meeting where I would be speaking that night.

Her report of our session is typical of the struggle people go through with the truth:

When I left I was disturbed and uncomfortable inside. I felt disapproved of, irritated, even critical. There was a lack of gentleness and warmth and few smiles. What I found I did not want to see. I am angry. I have used anger as a control strategy with my family. I have to be prepared to love my family when they are at their worst.

My problem is rooted in sin. Therefore, it is between me and the Lord. Awareness is not enough; it must lead to immediate repentance and cleansing through forgiveness. As much as I must be emptied of anger, I must also be filled with God's love. All this talk of sin and repentance makes me feel very bad. This is unwelcome. Henry Brandt is less gentle than God. He speaks of being wholly responsible for my own sin—not people involved, not circumstnces, not poor little me. Just something between me and God.

Am I still clinging to the cushion of "If my parents had only"? If I am honest, I have to say yes. This idea is easy enough to accept intellectually but very hard as it relates to experience and feeling. Something in me does not want to hear this.

After she attended two public meetings, she sent me this letter:

I have today seen how anger has been my mainstay all these years—a defense of sorts, often the only thing that kept me standing.

I have today seen how afraid I am to let it go. I began to see that yesterday—how the fear and the anger go together and why I could not let go of them.

I have today, by faith in the Lord Jesus, given Him that crutch. I have a picture of myself standing, swaying, and feeling terribly vulnerable and afraid—yet excited too. I know by faith that I can walk without that crutch. Love is stronger than anything. My anger was a wretched, impoverished make-do/counterfeit—the best I could come up with, but hopelessly inadequate. By faith in Jesus I can stand, walk, run forward in the power of love. I am healed. I am changed. I can love.

I have today remembered how operative anger has always been in my life—yet unadmitted (like the Theater of the Emotions). I have always been ready to be angry as a first response to anything negative or hard. Anything I could not handle. Anything that threatened me in any way, in fact. Hence all the criticism. I have always been quick to burn with anger and indignation on behalf of others, too. And behind that anger went fear—fear of everything, mostly. And the final, rotten deception: a fear of letting go of the very thing that was causing me so much trouble—anger. Fear=depression.

I thank God that He has brought me to this place. I face the future with some apprehension, but knowing more clearly than I have ever known that God is with me. God is for me. God besets me before and behind and has His hand on my shoulder. God loves me; and He makes me new. I do not need anger. He is my protection, my Rock, my Fortress, my Stronghold—and I can run into Him any time I want to or need to. He is my Father. This is what a Father is. This is who the Lord Jesus has led me to.

I expect I will fall down a lot as I learn to walk again. But that hand will have me safe—

though he fall, he shall not be utterly cast down; For the LORD upholds him with His hand.

Ps. 37:24

◆

6

Counseling in the Body of Christ

Discipling has many faces in the local church. Small groups, large groups, men's groups, women's groups, youth groups, and one-on-one are some of the different formats of discipling. Discipling and counseling go hand-in-hand.

The focus of counseling in the church should be discipleship. Discipleship includes walking with a person through their perceived problems, such as marriage, parenting, and stress-disorders. Helping persons examine and reorder their life in light of Scripture is the goal of discipleship and biblical counseling.

In the pages that follow, I will share my experiences of counseling in the local church. Whether you are a pastor, layperson, or biblical counselor, you can help others look to God for help. You may not use identical methods, but several elements must always be taken into consideration.

Four Counseling Considerations

1. Most Christians come to see their pastor or other member of the church after they have explored other avenues. For example, marriage and family therapists, psychiatrists, psychologists, Christian counselors, and group therapy.
2. Often, the person simply wants someone to listen and sympathize with his situation. People tend to want suggested change on behalf of those who live closest to them but not for themselves.
3. Christians expect counseling to take a long time. They will come to see you for as long as necessary or until you say something they do not want to hear.
4. Some people refuse to be comforted.

Considering these elements, how is a pastor/counselor to prepare for the encounter? After all, most counselees have been exposed to several kinds of counseling. What do you have to offer that is different? The simplicity of God's Word contains everything needed for Christians to return to a Spirit-controlled life. God will give the pastor or counselor all the wisdom needed through His Word and Spirit. God's wisdom will enable you to share His answer to the counselee's need.

The Pastor/Counselor's Preparation

1. Make sure there is no unconfessed sin in your life. You can do this by scanning chapter 3 and by using the chart on page 42 as a mirror. This chart is based on Mark 7:21–23; Romans 1:28–31; Galatians 5:19–21; Ephesians 4:25–31; and 2 Timothy 3:1–5. Scan the right-hand column. As you do, ask the Lord to show you any sin in your life. You can be adding to this list as the Lord sheds light on your path through Bible study and listening to people tell you their

experiences. Make sure that your additions can be referenced by Scripture.

2. Confess any known sin and by faith receive the cleansing you are promised.

3. Run your eye down the left-hand column. If you are clean in heart, you are now eligible to claim the fullness of the Spirit by faith.

4. Remember Jesus' promise:

> "I will ask the Father and he will give you another Counselor to be with you forever—the Spirit of truth."
>
> John 14:16–17, NIV

Ask the Lord to fill you with that Spirit of truth as you listen to the person's story you are about to hear.

5. Your plan is to listen to this person's story until a violation of a biblical principle comes to your mind.

6. Continue to listen until the person's story confirms your judgment and the person agrees (e.g., He is a very angry man and hates his wife).

7. Let him look at a biblical mirror (chart 1). It may help him identify some sin he is not even thinking about.

8. You must judge when the person is ready to face sin in his life. If the person accepts the truth (anger and hate is sin), it becomes his own truth. If he repents—admits his sin, seeks forgiveness and cleansing, asks for filling and control of the Spirit—you can move on. If not, you are stalled until he does.

9. If a person repents, he should be encouraged to approach God on his own when needed.

10. Get him started (alone or in a group) in *The Heart of the Problem* workbook (Broadman & Holman, © 1995).

11. Follow up. Make a date for the next appointment.

12. Remember, there were three involved in that interview: the counselee, the Holy Spirit, and you. Reflect a moment and recall how God led you.

Daily walking in a love relationship with Jesus Christ is essential preparation for pastoral discipleship. Your mind must be the instrument through which God shares His wisdom with the counselee.

> Do not be conformed to this world, but be transformed by the renewing of your mind.
>
> Rom. 12:2

Ask as many questions as possible that require scriptural answers. Once you have prepared your heart and mind, then prepare by having the necessary tools for discipling. I suggest you have the following available:

- ◆ Your Bible
- ◆ Spirit-Controlled vs. Sin-Controlled handout (p. 42)
- ◆ *The Heart of the Problem* workbook
- ◆ Listening Sheet (see appendix)

These four tools should be all you will need to help the person return to God.

How to Begin

If you do not know the person or persons well, get to know them. Ask them how they sensed God brought them to your church and to this particular session. As they talk, take notes on your listening sheet.

Ask them why they have come to see you.

Have them share their personal testimony. If you are going to approach them as a Christian, you had better make sure they are Christians.

Listen for biblical principles that are violated. Ask God to give you wisdom and discernment as they are talking. Stop and help them examine violated biblical principles.

Many Christians think they know what their problem is but they do not consider it sin. In fact, if you ask them, "What is the problem?" most will share their situation that troubles them. Their perspective often relates to "someone" or "something" they think is their problem.

I have intentionally asked this question to hundreds of people: "Do you have any unconfessed sin in your life?"

Answering that question is simple for some Christians. "No," they would say. "I prayed this morning and asked God to forgive me of my sin."

Doors are now open for you to share.

Ask them to listen as you give them background information that will be critical in dealing with their problem.

Case Study: John and Kathy

John and Kathy have been telling you their problem. Kathy begins by sharing that she is tired of living with John. They have been married for two years. She has discovered that John is not the person she thought he was. Kathy claims she cannot trust him anymore. John looks at other women, he lies, and he is deceitful.

Proceeding to tell about John, Kathy states that he attends a love and sex addiction support group, a low self-esteem support group, and sees a psychiatrist weekly. Now John wants to see a pastor too!

This is the time to ask Kathy for examples of what causes her to distrust him. Then, ask John to explain why he is attending support groups and seeing a psychiatrist. A Bible passage would help at this time:

"Nothing outside a man can make him 'unclean' by going into him. Rather it is what comes out of a man that makes him 'unclean.' For from within, out of men's hearts, come evil thoughts, sexual immorality, theft, murder, adultery, greed, malice, deceit, lewdness, envy, slander, arrogance and folly. All these evils come from inside and make a man 'unclean.'"

Mark 7:15–16; 21–23, NIV

Kathy is angry and openly displays the anger. Both John and Kathy claim they know Jesus Christ personally. Their anger, lust, and deception are obvious, based on their own testimony. When do you share biblical insights? As the Lord gives you wisdom.

Time to Use Your Bible

Begin by sharing share with them an important statement Jesus made. Read Mark 7:20–23 to them. Then simply ask the couple, "Jesus said that what comes out of your mouth or life proceeds from where?"

Wait for their response. "The heart."

"If anger, bitterness, or lust comes out, where did it come from?"

"The heart."

"If it comes from the heart, it is sin. If the problem is sin, there is no human remedy. No counselor, pastor, or friend can get rid of sin. But, if sin is your problem, it is the simplest thing in the world to deal with. Why? Because Jesus came for the express purpose of dealing with sin."

God's Word says:

"She will bring forth a Son, and you shall call His name JESUS, for He will save His people from their sins."

Matt. 1:21

Sin is simple to deal with from God's perspective but not easy from our perspective.

Then share with them the difference in the world's way versus God's way of dealing with their problem. The world would tell John that he has an addiction. As long as John will attend the love and sex addiction group therapy, he can manage his problem. The world offers relief, which feels great when you get it, but you must remember that relief is not a cure. The world cannot tell you how to get rid of anger, jealousy, bitterness, lust, or drunkenness, but the world can help you manage the problem.

The world's counsel may be, "There is nothing wrong with jealousy or bitterness. I have that in my life too." This makes it OK in their eyes. The world might ask you to "talk it out," "work it off, "play it off," "listen to music," or "release it." The "problems" have never been compared to God's Word. To the world, drunkenness is a disease that can at best only be managed. To God, it is sin that can be cleansed.

Jesus did not die and was not raised from the grave to provide relief. He provides a cure. Dr. Henry Blackaby once shared with me that Jesus did not come to teach the lame man how to adjust to his crutches. Jesus came to offer a real cure.

The world says John has an addiction to sex. God says that he has lust of the eyes and flesh. The world calls the problem an addiction; God says it is sin.

The world spends years to offer careful guidance to the problem, but Christians say one simply needs to repent. The world believes their way is kind and the Christian's ways are harsh.

Look at the deception of this world's philosophy. The world says they will help you through months or years of counsel. How many people are patient enough to last months or years in the middle of a crisis? Not many. I believe God is more merciful than the world. He offers a complete cure to life's problems.

Understanding this, share with John and Kathy the list of Spirit-Controlled vs. Sin-Controlled living (p. 42). As they look at the list, share with them that the list came from Scripture, not from the minds of men. God's Word is powerful. When John and Kathy look at the sins of the mind, emotions, mouth, and behavior, God points out their problem.

Kathy says that God quickly revealed that she is angry, unforgiving, unloving, bitter, and resentful. She knew her husband had sin but now knows that she also has sin in her life. John admits that he has deceit, lust, and unfaithfulness in his life.

Finally, they are making progress. If John makes right his relationship with God, and Kathy does the same, will they be in right relationship with one another? They agree that would be true, but how does that happen?

Moment of Truth

Questions which must be answered are:
1. Do you want to change?
2. Are you willing to use God's plan for change?
If they are, a cure is to come. John and Kathy began to weep and respond to God.

John and Kathy Repent

Have John and Kathy repented of their sins? Not yet. Even though they have not repented, they are in agreement that their marriage is not their problem—their heart is.

Proceed to give them two assignments. List these assignments on your listening sheet (see appendix).

"First, I want you to leave my office and find a place for each of you to get alone with God. Share with God the condition of your heart and that you desire a real cleansing and filling of His Spirit. Repent according to the process we discussed.

"Second, you are to obtain a copy of *The Heart of the Problem* and work through it one day at a time. As God speaks to you through His Word, share with one another what God is saying to you.

"Third, come back after you have done your assignments. If you do not do your homework, do not come back to see me. Assignments completed will let me know if you want to repent. Would a person spend time and money going to a medical doctor and then not follow his prescription?"

John and Kathy receive the words and leave. The next week they come back for a follow-up visit. Kathy begins by saying that John is not the same man and she is not the same woman. They say they had tried all of the world's ways with no success. God has completely turned their lives around in one week! You might think that is impossible. God has always specialized in doing the impossible!

What is their next assignment? There are two. First, have them keep doing what they did in the previous session. Second, they are to get involved in Bible study with other couples, come to church, listen to God's Word preached, and pray with others.

Five Steps of Repentance

Like driving, repentance is a process which needs to be walked through, step by step. Repentance is rare but brings a cure when enacted.

Learning to drive a car with a manual transmission is difficult at first. It seems as though the eyes, hands, and feet will never work together at the same time. Driving seems to require many steps. However, after you become experienced, you drive the car without thinking through the steps. The following steps will help you understand the process of repentance.

Step 1: "Lord, I Am Wrong!"

Suppose my son came to me and said he had not cleaned his room for 365 days in a row. Can you imagine the result of his wrong action? Yet it is very difficult for him to admit he is wrong. He may not consider his actions wrong. However, he knows I have told him that in this house it is wrong. My son finally admits his wrongs and then says, "See you later, Dad. I am going to the beach." His words are right, but his actions are unchanged. Why? Because he does not want to change. Admitting he is wrong needs to match his behavior. Many Christians never go any further than this because they do not agree they are wrong.

Did King David know he was wrong when he committed adultery and murder? Yes! Why did he remain unchanged? Because his wrongs had not reached his heart. Later, when confronted by the prophet Nathan, David saw his wrongs against God.

Step 2: "Lord, I Am Sorry!"

Suppose my son states on day 366, "Dad, I know it is wrong to neglect cleaning my room because you said it was wrong. I am sorry I have not cleaned it because I know it upsets our relationship. See you later, I am going to the beach." Sorrow like this is certainly not like the sorrow in Scripture.

> Now I rejoice, not that you were made sorry, but that your sorrow led to repentance. For you were made sorry in a godly manner, that you might suffer loss from us in nothing. For godly sorrow produces repentance leading to salvation, not to be regretted; but the sorrow of the world produces death. For observe this very thing, that you sorrowed in a godly manner: What diligence it produced in

you, what clearing of yourselves, what indignation, what fear, what vehement desire, what zeal, what vindication!

2 Cor. 7:9–11

Many people are sorry they got caught or sorry that a relationship has been harmed, but they do not have a godly sorrow that leads to change. Sorry-I-got-caught sorrow will not change a wounded relationship. This is worldly sorrow. It ignores the problem or gives a defense and brings death to a relationship.

Remember, godly sorrow is not repentance but leads to repentance.

Step 3: "Lord, Will You Forgive Me?"

Let's suppose on day 367 my son comes to me and says, "Dad, I have not cleaned my room in 367 days. I am wrong. I am sorry. Will you forgive me?" Well, what do you think I would do as a parent? I would say, "Sure, I forgive you." I am thinking he is going to clean his room. He says, "Thanks, Dad. It feels so good to be forgiven. I do not feel so guilty now. See you later, I am going to the beach!"

Many Christians do the same thing. They admit their sorrow. They admit their wrongs. They ask God to forgive them, but they go on about life as though nothing has changed. You ask, "How can that happen?"

Has God ever convicted you of the same sin over and over? You pray, "God, will You forgive me? I have not cleaned my room." For many Christians it might be, "I have not been reading Your Word. Would You forgive me? Lord, would You help me to be obedient? Thank You, God."

After praying at the altar, you go back and sit in the pew, and two weeks later nothing has changed. Your life is still the same. There has been no repentance. It has simply been an acknowledgment that you are wrong and that you want to be back in right relationship with God. You desire to have a renewed relationship with God without ever changing your life.

Step 4: "Lord, Cleanse Me!"

My son comes to me and says, "I have not cleaned my room in 368 days in a row. I know it is wrong, and I am sorry. Would you forgive me."

I say, "Oh yes, son, I forgive you."

He says, "Dad, I want to go beyond that. I really mean business today. I want a total cleansing. I want you to save me from my self. I want you to cleanse me from my past actions. Dad, I do not want you to hold these past 368 days against me. Would you just wipe the slate clean?"

I say, "Yes, son. I will do that."

"Great, Dad, I am going to clean my room right now."

He has come to the place where there is truly a godly sorrow. He walks to his room, but he finds the same thing that many of you find after you have been living and dealing with the same sin of anger, jealousy, envy, bitterness, or resentment for ten, fifteen, or maybe twenty years. He knows his heart and his relationship with his father has been renewed, but his character from the past is still there. His room is still dirty. He has to face it.

So my son comes back down the hall and says, "Dad, I made a mess. My eyes are open. I see the result of my lifestyle and I need help. I do not have the ability in and of myself to clean my room. Will you help me?"

I say, "Oh yes, son, I will be glad to help you."

God is just a repentant prayer away all the time.

Step 5: "Lord, Empower Me!"

My son looks at the room and says, "Dad, I need a vacuum cleaner, a broom, dust polish, and any other things that it takes to clean my room. Quite honestly, I am out of practice. I have not done this in a long time. I want to clean the room and keep it clean. Thanks for giving me a change of heart, Dad. Will you help me clean my room? I cannot do it by myself."

Many Christians miss this step when they are wanting to see a real change in their life. Why? Because we live in a world where even if we do admit our sin, we will say, "If you will just tell me what is wrong, I will correct it. Please show me my problem and I will fix it." So, Christians get on their knees on Sunday and say, "God forgive me! I have been angry. My heart is filled with anger. Every time I get around my boss at work, I get angry. Every time he speaks to me, I get angry."

Then they get up from their knees and say, "I know what the problem is. It is anger. I am determined when I go to work tomorrow that whatever my boss does, I will not get angry." Guess what happens? They get angry! They are depending upon their ability to act like a Christian instead of being a Christian. There is a vast difference between the two.

They may go to God and say, "Look at me! I am angry. I cannot even help myself. God, You have cleansed me of my anger. But if I go back in my own strength to live like I think You want me to, I will miss the mark. God, will You fill me with the fruit of Your Spirit and empower me with the fruit of Your Spirit so that I can live Your way and not mine? Please give me love for my boss who does things that reveal my heart. Please give me love for my spouse. Give me peace in my heart that passes all understanding. Give me joy instead of my depression." This will bring a cure.

◆

7

The Role of Repentance in Counseling

Have you ever been in prayer groups where God's people would pray something like this: "Oh God, please send an awakening to our land?"

Many of God's people have faithfully prayed this for years and yet have not seen spiritual awakening in America. Why? Spiritual awakening carries with it a requirement of God's people. That requirement is repentance. God's people must repent of sin and become the people that He intended for us to be. I am convinced that, when this happens, we will see renewal in our nation.

Dealing with Sin

What does dealing with sin have to do with counseling? Remember, counseling is simply taking the Word of God and helping a person examine his heart in light of the Bible. If that examination reveals sin, repentance is the only road to the cure. If thousands of Christians practice counseling that refuses to deal with sin, Christians will see no need to repent and return to God. If they do not turn to God, there will be no spiritual awakening.

You may blame our nation's decline on drug dealers, on abortionists, and on murderers and rapists. God's people tend to blame unbelievers for the condition of their nation. But our nation is not declining because lost people are getting worse. Throughout the Old and New Testament the condition of a nation always depended on the condition of God's people. Therefore, what is happening in your community and mine, in our state and our nation, can be traced to the apathy of God's people.

Long ago God revealed the key to personal and national revival to Solomon:

> "If My people who are called by My name will humble themselves, and pray and seek My face, and turn from their wicked ways, then I will hear from heaven, and will forgive their sin and heal their land."
>
> 2 Chron. 7:14

Jeremiah speaks clearly to the unfaithfulness of God's people. He declares their unfaithfulness is sin. Though this message was directed to God's chosen people of the Old Testament, it also points to us today—"If My people." We tend to think that our unfaithfulness to God is simply a time when we have strayed slightly away from God. Failing to follow God does not seem as wrong as getting drunk, lying, or committing adultery. We continue to minimize the seriousness of our unfaithfulness and say that it is not that critical. But we excuse our actions by saying we have just relaxed a little too much and have not been faithful enough in our walk with Him. God's people must awaken to the truth that every sin is always serious. It is sin for His people to be unfaithful to Him.

People or Just Statistics?

Henry and Marilynn Blackaby spent three weeks in East and South Africa, where they ministered to about four hundred missionaries. After returning, Henry shared with me of the brokenness our missionaries and the people of East and South Africa had experienced. The missionaries in Rwanda were recently forced to flee. These missionaries had been in Rwanda for years. Now, everything was gone except their lives and the clothes on their backs.

In the 1930s there had been a sweeping revival and spiritual awakening across Rwanda. God's Spirit again moved through the land in the 1970s, opening wide the door for missionaries to minister to the people. Many Rwandans accepted Christ, and many were called to the gospel ministry. All seemed to be going well. Then came tragedy. History shows that every time a great awakening has moved through a country, there has also followed a great catastrophe.

Our missionaries were broken, saying, "God had given us such a ripe time for harvest in the 1970s and up until the last few years. Did we fail to make the most of it? Were we too complacent, saying, 'Everything is going pretty well right now'?" Their depth of grief moved them to see life from God's perspective.

Not long after this 1994 Rwanda tragedy, I came across an article about what was happening there. It discussed the feelings of many Americans who were not sure they wanted the United States to get involved. The writer shared that if a story had come across the news about one particular family in Rwanda who was murdered unmercifully, our hearts would have gone out to that family. But now that more than a million people have been killed, it was just a statistic.

The week earlier, the writer and his wife lost their seventeen-year-old son in death. They felt the pain and misery of losing their son. He then asked why Americans think that even though Rwandans look different, dress differently, and are on a different level socially and economically, that they would grieve any less when their children are killed.

Many American Christians are past feeling. It is sad when we come to the place that the calamities of our day have become, in our eyes and minds, no more than simple statistics. Many minds are filled with false thinking and false hope about what is happening in our nation.

Listen urgently to what the Spirit of God is saying to His people. I pray that our hearts would be changed and that our view would not be, "Should we afford the expense to help the Rwandans?" If we continue to hold that attitude in America, we will pay a great price for it. Oh that God would break our hearts over the condition of our lives in relationship to Him! Oh that the people of God would repent of unfaithfulness to Him! Jeremiah voiced the heart cry of a concerned believer:

> My heart is broken within me. All my bones tremble. I am like a drunken man, like a man overcome by wine because of the LORD and his holy words.
>
> Jer. 23:9, NIV

When a Holy God speaks to His people, it is not a time for rejoicing. It is a time for a solemn heart searching. There is a time for rejoicing, but there is also a time for brokenness. Jeremiah laid the blame on God's people. Being confronted with the condition of our heart brings a very solemn spirit.

> The land is full of adulterers; for because of a curse the land mourns. The pleasant places of the wilderness are dried up.
>
> Jer. 23:10

And sadly, God's servants have failed. The people are in this condition because they have been unfaithful to God and have followed after other gods. God removed them from their homeland and left a barren land.

False Hopes

Many are offering false hopes to save our society. To the drunk, the world says it is not his fault; it is a disease or an addiction. He cannot control himself. Society must save him! Society says, "We want to help you. We have groups to support you. We will help you manage this problem." Why does this reveal false hope? Because the same groups will say to the alcoholic, "You will always be an alcoholic. You will never get rid of this, but we can teach you how to manage it." God is much more gracious than that. He offers a cure—Jesus.

We have listened to the message of this world so long that we can no longer distinguish the difference between false hope and the Word of God. What would God say in our day concerning alcoholism? In the New and Old Testament it is never referred to as alcoholism. It is never referred to as a disease. It is always referred to as sin. If alcoholism is sin, there is no human remedy. Thanks be to God that His Son Jesus offers full and abundant life, not the condemnation of an incurable disorder.

Yet we as human beings are offering false hope in our world by using a worldly way of thinking. To the person addicted to some substance we say, "We'll teach you how to manage this, but you can never get rid of it, for if you ever get around it again it will come right back on you. You see, this is a disease for which we have no cure." However, if alcoholism is what God says it is—drunkenness—there is a cure. Jesus Christ can cure the alcoholic. He can remove the sin from a person. You simply must take the Word of God and decide whether you believe the Word or the world.

During a recent year I counseled almost a hundred families who came to church every week, yet their marriages were falling apart. Most of these people had already been to every other source looking for help—the marriage therapist, the family therapist, support groups, even to studies within our own church. They had been to psychologists, psychiatrists, and counselors. Is it wrong to turn to these sources for help? The answer depends on whether or not they are based on the world or the Word.

People often come to me and other biblical counselors as a last resort. "We need help in our marriage," they say. But their marriage is not their problem. Their problem is personal sin. The world would say, "Kerry, you're being too harsh, telling people that the problem in their marriage is sin and that repentance is the solution. You need to help them work through these everyday struggles in their marriage. It may take months of convincing them to stay together and work it out. You should offer them two years of counseling to get them back in shape." That is the world's approach.

I believe that offers a false hope. If the wife's heart is right toward God, and the husband's heart is right toward God, their marriage is open to God's healing. Any advice not based on the Word of God will bring false hope.

> This is what the Lord Almighty says: "Do not listen to what the prophets are prophesying to you; they fill you with false hopes. They speak visions from their own minds, not from the mouth of the Lord."
>
> Jer. 23:16

The world is doing the best they know how to offer help. However, it is from their own minds that they offer wisdom. According to the verse above, the very same thing took place in Jeremiah's day. We as Christians in our day must decide whether God's Word supersedes everything else on the bookstore shelf.

I walked into a bookstore in downtown Atlanta, just to see what was on the shelves. I went to the "Self-Help" section. Would you believe that this section was almost the largest in the entire store? There were helps to improve one's self, one's attitudes, one's health, one's job satisfaction. As I looked at some of these, I began to see a picture of the false thinking of our day.

Self-gratification is another false hope we have in our day—anything that gratifies me, that improves me, no matter what it does to people around me.

> They continually say to those who despise me, "The LORD has said: 'You shall have peace'; and to everyone who walks according to the dictates of his own heart, they say, 'No evil shall come upon you.'"
>
> Jer. 23:17

Our lives have been so saturated by the media and the teachings of our day to believe our salvation is within ourselves, our attitudes, and positive thinking. We have spent more time studying these sources than we have spent searching the Word of God. As a result, we get mixed up about right from wrong, true from false. We do not know enough about God and His Word to know His answer to our personal and social problems.

As a result, hardness of heart comes to the Christian. How do I know? Why is it that divorce, teenage suicide, AIDS, and adultery have come into the church yet many have no grief in their heart?

If one member suffers, all the members suffer with it; or if one member is honored, all the members rejoice with it.

1 Cor. 12:26

Unfaithful to God

Broken marriages are one of the critical hurts in the church. Families are breaking apart every single day among believers who say Christ is the center of their lives. Recently I realized that not only are prophets teaching false hopes, but many Christians are living false thinking, and no one challenges it!

Here is some of the false thinking:

- If my mate would just act better, our marriage would get better.

- If my mate would just start changing, reading a few more of these self-help books, and become a better communicator, then our marriage would get right back on track.

- If my husband wouldn't leave his shoes in the middle of the room all the time, I would be a better wife.

- If my wife could cook better, I would be a more supportive husband.

Christian! The reason our marriages are falling apart like they are is not primarily because of our unfaithfulness to one another but to God. Faithfulness to Him will bring a faithfulness to one another. God wants to put marriages back together. God is sickened by the pettiness of the things that destroy marriages. He wants us to love Him with all our heart, soul, and mind. Out of a Christian heart overflowing with love for God will flow love enough to heal a marriage.

Have you ever wondered how Christian marriages survived before the invention of the printing press? How did

Christians live without all of today's books? Do you think God knew that He would need to provide something in the hearts of Christians to make their marriage better? Of course He did! He was to produce in them the fruit of the Spirit—love, joy, peace, and long-suffering—which make relations possible and happy!

The Spirit of God is available today to every broken-hearted Christian. My heart aches over many I have counseled who were living in unfaithfulness to God. Christians must see that sin is not primarily against one another but toward God.

> The heart is deceitful above all things, and desperately wicked.
>
> Jer. 17:9

Jeremiah is saying to the people of God, "Oh, people of God, come back to follow what the Word of the Lord God says."

False Prophets

We have believed what the the world is saying to us. Go ahead and act the way you do to your spouse, your boss, your children. Treat your parents the way you want. You have a right to be yourself and to act your way. But God says:

> "But which of them [prophets] has stood in the council of the LORD to see or to hear his word? Who has listened and heard his word?"
>
> Jer. 23:18, NIV

What does God have to say about all of this? Who has listened and heard His word? Through Jeremiah, God said,

"But if they had stood in My counsel, caused My people to hear My words, then would have turned them from their evil way and from the evil of their doings."

Jer. 23:22

A great question to ask in our day is, "If the world is right in their counsel, why are all the evidences of social sickness becoming more and more frequent and deadly?" People are not turning from their evil ways. You will know whether a word is from God if, when applied to your life, it makes a change in your life. You say, "Well, I've tried that and nothing happened." I did not say that you should *attempt* to do some things. You must apply God's Word to your life by the power of the Holy Spirit, working in and through you. When you do that, it will turn you from your evil ways.

Our newspapers and media reveal alarming statistics of abortions, divorces, teenage deaths, alcoholism, drug abuse, and mass murders. In light of this, ask yourself this question, "Is all the help people are seeking after today turning them from their wicked ways?"

"How long will this be in the heart of the prophets who prophesy lies? Indeed they are prophets of the deceit of their own heart, make My people forget My name by their dreams which everyone tells his neighbor, as their fathers forgot My name for Baal. The prophet who has a dream, let him tell a dream: and he who has My word, let him speak My word faithfully."

Jer. 23:26–28

If you use the world's method to try to heal your life, you will end up in failure. If you obey the Word of God, what a great cure you will find! There is a song that says, "Grace is greater than all our sins." This does not just mean that grace is so powerful it can forgive us of all our sin. Grace, when it is practiced in your life, will bring greater joy than all the sin of the world. Grace is greater than sin. Grace will bring a heart for God. A heart for God will bring a love and respect for His Word. God's Word will bring adjustments to our life.

> "Is not My word like a fire?" says the LORD, "and like a hammer that breaks the rock in pieces?"
>
> Jer. 23:29

When husbands and wives get into an argument, one can leave the room and get away from the other's voice. In fact, we can block another person's words out of our mind. When God speaks to your heart, you cannot run from it. You could drive all day long and still not get away from what God has spoken to your heart. His Word is like fire, like a hammer that breaks the stoniest heart in pieces. God says,

> "I will give them an undivided heart and put a new spirit in them; I will remove from them their heart of stone and give them a heart of flesh. Then they will follow my decrees and be careful to keep my laws. They will be my people, and I will be their God."
>
> Ezek. 11:19–20, NIV

God will give a heart of flesh that will care for what is happening in our world, a heart of flesh that says, "I am concerned about my marriage to the extent that I will repent of how I have been acting, for this very action shows my unfaithfulness to God.

> "Therefore," declares the LORD, "I am against the prophets who steal from one another words supposedly from me."
>
> Jer. 23:30

What a message for our day. There are a lot of books on the shelf that appear to be Christian. Many are filled with words that are supposedly from God. However, if they are not based on the Bible, they are not from God.

You should be very careful when you say, "Thus sayeth the Lord" because if it is not what God said in His Word, judgment will come upon what you said to the people of God.

> "Yes," declares the LORD, "I am against the prophets who wag their own tongues and yet declare, 'The Lord declares.'"
>
> Jer. 23:31

The desire of these authors is that you experience the fullness of a faithful relationship with God. When you come into a right relationship with Him and see sin for how terrible it really is, when you honestly repent of that sin, you will experience the mighty grace of God that brings relief and cure in your life like nothing else you have ever known. God knows your heart. He wants you to be faithful to Him, and nothing less than faithfulness to God will bring victory in those difficult areas of your life.

Faithfulness to God is a prerequisite for sharing the Word of God with another Christian. When you are faithful, it allows God to use you to share the positive message of repentance.

◆

8

Feeding on the Word

This chapter came together after spending two days seeing eight different counselees. All eight were well housed, well educated, well fed, and with ample income, yet they were mean, angry, and disgruntled people. According to them, God had singled each one of them out to vent His wrath on them. The people in this world, especially Christians, were all selfish hypocrites. Not one of the eight was involved in any consistent Bible study.

I needed to take a spiritual bath. I thumbed through a collection of "diamonds" (Bible verses) that helped me check my thinking process and make sure my mind was working according to my guide book, the Bible.

God's Promises

Move as slow or as fast as you like through these comments. You may not like some of them. Perhaps you can improve on them.

> Great peace have those who love Your law, and nothing causes them to stumble.
>
> Ps. 119:165

Do you believe that? It will shape your counseling. Will you mislead a child or a young man who comes to you by agreeing that they could not help what they did? That anybody in their spot would do the same thing? That is not comfort, that is cruelty. Are they neglecting Bible study?

> Delight yourself also in the Lord and He shall give you the desires of your heart.
>
> Ps. 37:4

Frustration is a warning to check up on your spirit. In all tenderness and kindness, these people must realize that the way they are responding to what God is allowing in their lives is very questionable. They do not need to walk out of a room unhappy. Before they get to the end of the corridor they can have peace.

> In perfect peace You will keep him whose mind is stayed on You because he trusts in You.
>
> Isa. 26:3

What a hopeful verse that we can so easily ignore. Perfect trust is rare.

> The work of righteousness will be peace, and the effect of righteousness, quietness and assurance forever.
>
> Isa. 32:17

Not having my own righteousness which comes from the law, but that which is through faith in Christ—the righteousness which is from God by faith.

Phil. 3:9

So if you think you are standing firm, be careful that you don't fall!

1 Cor. 10:12, NIV

We know the effects of righteousness are peace and joy and quietness and confidence. Right? But we must submit to help that is not our own.

Commit your works to the LORD, and your thoughts will be established.

Prov. 16:3

People say, "I cannot make up my mind." Why not? Then, what can you look for? Rebellion against what God is allowing in your life? Making up my mind is a battle that I know very well. To want God's will with all my heart all of the time is an experience that I have not yet achieved.

The LORD is my strength and my shield; my heart trusted in Him, and I am helped; therefore my heart greatly rejoices and with my song I will praise Him.

Ps. 28:7

This is the possibility of the Christian life. What short-circuits this kind of life? Environment, family background, education, wrong friends, unfortunate experience?

He who covers his sins will not prosper, but whoever confesses and forsakes them will have mercy.

Prov. 28:13

His own sin is the problem. What are his sins? Someone might respond, "I do not have any sins." Well, what else could be the trouble?

He who does not prosper is covering up some sin.

The heart is deceitful above all things and beyond cure. Who can understand it? "I the LORD search the heart and examine the mind, to reward a man according to his conduct, according to what his deeds deserve."

Jer. 17:9, NIV

You are in danger if you think of yourself otherwise.

We have much more respect for cancer or germs than we have for sin. You take proper precautions to keep yourself healthy, and you are perfectly willing to do it every day of your life until you die. Many of us as Christians, however, get careless about protecting ourselves from sin.

Behold the LORD's hand is not shortened, that it cannot save; nor His ear heavy, that it cannot hear. But your iniquities have separated you from your God; and your sins have hidden His face from you, so that He will not hear.

Isa. 59:1–2

Biblical Standards

We have some standard questions that we ask people who come to see us.

- Do you go to church regularly?

- Do you read the Bible regularly?

- Do you pray regularly?

Many answer yes to all of these. What could be wrong? It is not what they prayed about; it is what they do not pray about. It is not what they read in the Bible; it is what they do not read in the Bible. The problem is not whether they attend church. It is whether they worship when they get there.

This is *not* a valid assumption: If you read the Bible and pray every day, you will keep out of trouble. These can be rituals. Two men went up to the temple to pray. One said, "God, look at me! Is it not wonderful that You have me?" The other one said, "God, be merciful unto me a sinner!" Who went away justified? They both went up there to pray.

> Who shall separate us from the love of Christ? Shall tribulation or distress, or persecution, or famine, or nakedness, or peril or sword?
>
> Rom. 8:35

What can? Your wickedness and your sin can. It comes back to you, does it not?

> As it is written: "For Your sake we are killed all day long; we are accounted as sheep for the slaughter." Yet, in all these things we are more than conquerors through Him who loved us.
>
> Rom. 8:36–37

You must experience more and more of this if you are to be a counselor who leads people to the fountain that will give them victory.

> For I am persuaded that neither death nor life, nor angels nor principalities, nor powers, nor things present nor things to come, nor height nor depth, nor other created thing, shall be able to separate us from the love of God which is in Christ Jesus our Lord.
>
> Rom. 8:38–39

None of these things can separate us from the love of God.
Jesus said,

> "A new commandment I give to you, that you love one another."
>
> John 13:34

Can you think of somebody you do not like? That is bad. Are you willing to live with it? You had better look out. You might fall flat on your face one of these days.

You are not alone:

No temptation has overtaken you except such as is common to man.

1 Cor. 10:13

We are all in the same boat. The sinfulness of sin.

We know that the law is spiritual; but I am unspiritual, sold as a slave to sin.

Rom. 7:14, NIV

Quite a statement of helplessness!

I do not understand what I do. For what I want to do I do not do, but what I hate I do. And if I do what I do not want to do, I agree that the law is good. As it is, it is no longer I myself who do it, but it is sin living in me.

Rom. 7:15–17, NIV

No matter what standard you set, you will not live up to it. You say the Bible's standards are high—I am not quarreling with that. Set up your own standard. You will not live up to it. I do not know anything about you, but I know the Bible. I have no reason to change my bias because I have yet to see anyone to whom this does not apply.

I know that nothing good lives in me, that is, in my sinful nature. For I have the desire to do what is good, but I cannot carry it out. For what I do is not the good I want to do; no, the evil I do not want to do–this I keep doing. Now if I do what I do not want to do, it is no longer I who do it, but it is sin living in me that does it.

Rom. 7:18–20, NIV

Your job as a counselor is to identify specific sins in that person's life.

> I find this law at work: When I want to do good, evil is right there with me. For in my inner being I delight in God's law; but I see another law at work in the members of my body, waging war against the law of my mind and making me a prisoner of the law of sin at work within my members.
>
> Rom. 7:21–23, NIV

This is why discussion has its limitations and why agreements fall down. Because we cannot live up to them. At times, we keep our agreements outwardly but our hearts have departed from them. Often people say, "My wife does not have the slightest idea of this. Please do not tell her." Their hearts have departed. I can walk into church, but my mind is not always there.

> The wicked are like the troubled sea, when it cannot rest, whose waters cast up mire and dirt. "There is no peace," says my God, "for the wicked."
>
> Isa. 57:20–21

There is no peace to the wicked. Start looking for evidence of wickedness. I do not mean that you robbed a bank or committed murder. Jesus said that if you are angry at your brother, you have committed murder. What is the difference between being mildly annoyed and murder? It is a matter of degree. You just did not get mad enough.

Is that a valid statement? That will be a good one for you to chew on. I have been spelling out a principal. Now I want to get a little bit more specific.

Sin and the Law

> Whoever commits sin also commits lawlessness, and sin is lawlessness.
>
> 1 John 3:4

If it says that you should do it and you do not do it, you have sinned. Sin is transgression of the law. If it says you do not do it and you do, you have sinned. The law is something I cannot keep. I use it as a mirror every day, and I realize that I have fallen short.

One of my counselees has committed grand larceny—he stole a car. This young man went before the judge and the judge gave him a big speech about integrity and honesty. He walked out of that courtroom and stole another car. Did that boy ever pull the wool over my eyes! He is one of the smoothest liars I ever saw. Fooled me completely. He ended up in a detention home. Two days before I left, he tried to break out of there. "Should I love him? You do not decide "Should I, or should I not." You do, or you don't. Should I wait till he straightens up and then love him?

While we were still sinners, Christ died for us.

Rom. 5:8

Is it right to go thirty-five miles per hour through a twenty-five-mile-per-hour zone?

All wrongdoing is sin.

1 John 5:17, NIV

I do it. I am sure relieved when I get through that town. I say that is sin.

Anyone, then, who knows the good he ought to do and doesn't do it, sins.

James 4:17, NIV

The schemes of folly are sin.

Prov. 24:9

Sin is a bad condition, is it not? There is much that I do not understand in the Bible, but I understand this:

For rebellion is as the sin of witchcraft, and stubbornness is as iniquity and idolatry. Because you have rejected the word of the LORD, He also has rejected you from being king.

1 Sam. 15:23

Read Colossians 3:5–9; Mark 7:14; Titus 3:1–4; Ephesians 4:18–32; and Galatians 5:19. These are typical Bible verses that give you a working knowledge of sin so that you can compare it to the counselee's story.

The Normal Heart

Doctors know what a normal heart sounds like, so they can tell if you deviate from that normal heart. You must know what normal Christian living is if you can determine how far your counselee deviates from the norm. Is this how you do it in your office? If you dedicate yourself to this kind of a ministry, you will have a trail of grateful people to look back on. I hope I am giving you a picture of the sinfulness of sin. I hope I am giving you the horror of it. I hope you think it is as bad as cancer, and I hope you, if you have not, from this day on will make daily provision to keep watch over your soul. Paul said,

Not that we are sufficient of ourselves to think of anything as being from ourselves, but our sufficiency is from God.

2 Cor. 3:5

In the fourth chapter Paul writes, "we have this treasure in earthen vessels" (v. 7). I think that it is important that we remember from where our strength comes. When we have this power in our lives, we will respond as follows: "We are hard pressed on every side, yet not crushed" (v. 8).

Think back over your last year. Were you distressed? The Bible says that you can be troubled on every side. Did you ever have that much trouble? If you yielded to the Spirit of God in you, you were not distressed.

The psalmist says,

> I will both lie down in peace, and sleep; for You alone, O LORD, make me dwell in safety.

Ps. 4:8

People come in and say, "I have spent many sleepless nights over this problem." My response to that? "You are not appropriating what God has for you if you toss and turn and fuss and fret. Give your burdens to the Lord."

I don't mean to be indifferent. I mean to take advantage of our privileges. It would be ridiculous for me to push a car down the street when I can get in and ride. If you take on the law without the power, you are taking on a heavy burden. Perplexed yes, but not in despair.

> Persecuted, but not forsaken; struck down, but not destroyed—always carrying about in the body the dying of the Lord Jesus, that the life of Jesus also may be manifested in our body.

2 Cor. 4:9–10

It is good religion when you can enjoy trouble and good times both. One of the grandest opportunities of testimony for God that you will ever have is when you are in the most trouble. Sunday School teachers ask me once in a while what to do with a brat in their Sunday School class. The best teaching happens when kids look on while the problem child is being handled. That is a golden opportunity to teach those children how a Christian reacts toward a brat. Many Sunday School teachers act like a brat to their brats!

In the garden of Gethsemane Jesus reported to God that He had delivered God's words to the men that God gave to Him. Jesus sometimes referred to His words as food, water, and life.

"If anyone thirsts, let him come to Me and drink. He who believes in Me, as the Scripture has said, out of his heart will flow rivers of living water." But this He spoke concerning the Spirit, whom those believing in Him would receive; for the Holy Spirit was not yet given, because Jesus was not yet glorified.

John 7:37–39

"I am the bread of life."

John 6:35

"My food is to do the will of Him who sent Me, and to finish His work."

John 4:34

"The words that I speak to you are spirit, and they are life."

John 6:63

Those who obey His commands live in him, and he in them. And this is how we know that he lives in us: We know it by the Spirit he gave us.

1 John 3:24, NIV

Hunt for the Word of God

A biblical counselor needs to experience a continuous hunger and thirst for the Word and a continuous awareness of walking in the Spirit. The steady application of Jesus' words with the intent to live by them will produce a drive to give our flesh and blood (our life) in serving Him by sharing the living word that God gave to Jesus. He gave it to us by word and by His life. Now it is our turn to do the same. We are His ambassadors. The key is not just a knowledge of Scripture, but a relationship with the God of

Scripture. The Scriptures do not give life, Jesus does. As a starter, you can feed on these verses:

"Heaven and earth will pass away, but My words will by no means pass away."

Matt. 24:35

"Sanctify them by Your truth. Your word is truth."

John 17:17

"You are already clean because of the word which I have spoken to you."

John 15:3

"You are mistaken, not knowing the Scriptures nor the power of God."

Matt. 22:29

Here are other statements about the benefit of feeding on the Word.

Blessed are they who keep His testimonies, who seek Him with the whole heart!

Ps. 119:2

Your word I have hidden your word in my heart, that I might not sin against you.

Ps. 119:11

The entrance of Your words gives light; it gives understanding to the simple.

Ps. 119:130

I have more insight than all my teachers, for I meditate on your statutes. I have more understanding than the elders, for I obey your precepts.

Ps. 119:99–100, NIV

For in the gospel a righteousness from God is revealed, a righteousness that is by faith from first to last, just as it is written: "The righteous will live by faith."

Rom. 1:17, NIV

The word of God is living and powerful, and sharper than any two-edged sword, piercing even to the division of soul and spirit, and of joints and marrow, and is a discerner of the thoughts and intents of the heart.

Heb. 4:12

All Scripture is given by inspiration of God, and is profitable for doctrine, for reproof, for correction, for instruction in righteousness, that the man of God may be complete, thoroughly equipped for every good work.

2 Tim. 3:16–17

A biblical counselor loves God and His Word, the Bible. You might say he is addicted to partaking of it regularly. He loves to share biblical truth with others. He has a happy, relaxed, wholesome attitude toward life.

A wholesome life is based upon knowing and practicing biblical principles. Our centerpiece says it best:

To those who through the righteousness of our God and Savior Jesus Christ have received a faith as precious as ours: Grace and peace be yours in abundance through the knowledge of God and of Jesus our Lord. His divine power has given us everything we need for life and godliness through our knowledge of him who called us by his own glory and goodness. Through these he has given us his very great and precious promises, so that through them you may participate in the divine nature and escape the corruption in the world caused by evil desires.

2 Pet. 1:1–4, NIV

Focal Points

Food (the Word) and Water (the Holy Spirit) are necessary if the biblical counselor is to understand God's Word.

Two words—*biblical* and *counselor*—are interesting as they are put together. God's Word is the text used if any speech, book, or counseling is to be considered biblical. The word counsel means, "to consult, confide in, consider." If you are to be a biblical counselor, you must consult, confide in, and consider the person of Christ (truth) in the Bible. Therefore, one can assume that if one consults something other than the Bible for counseling, it ceases to be biblical counseling.

Saturating one's life in the Bible is a delight to the biblical counselor.

> But his delight is in the law of the LORD, and in His law he meditates day and night.
>
> Ps. 1:2

Daily reading, meditating, and study of the Word is necessary for a counselor to stay fresh in a relationship with the Word (Jesus). The Word is a person—Jesus (see John 1:1). A relationship on a day-by-day basis is necessary if you are to use the Truth to set self or others free (see John 8:31–32). There are two key subjects the biblical counselor needs to be well acquainted with: sin, and the spirit-filled life. If there is no sin, there is no need for Christ, the Word and Truth. If there is sin, the biblical counselor must have processed scriptural truth into life so that he can recognize sin when he sees it. Earlier Scripture references in this chapter are essential for a biblical counselor.

Is it possible to live a life filled with the Spirit of God? Absolutely! Why? That is the express purpose of Jesus' coming—to save His people from their sins.

◆

9

Teach Me to Grieve

Society expects bereaved people to be desperately unhappy and miserable. The better the relationship was to the deceased, the greater should be the grief. It seems that Christians expect the ministry of the Holy Spirit to shut down when someone in the family dies.

When someone dies, there are multiple relationships going on in addition to the death. We tend to assume that the grieving person's only problem is the death of someone. Grief is often mingled with other unresolved conflicts. However, the vignettes in this chapter illustrate how other events are going on at the same time the death occurs.

After forty years of counseling and teaching, I cannot recall a single person who requested help because life is working out perfectly and this person is fed up with a satisfied, contented life. Contentment is illusive. We think we have found the key to it and it slips away.

A crisis in life involving you directly or indirectly is like driving a car. If someone suddenly stops in front of you or swerves into your lane, it is over before you know it. You have already drawn upon your driving skills and reflexes, developed over a period of time.

Everyone hears or reads about various crises happening to people everyday. It is just news until a crisis comes close to home, until something happens to you or someone close to you. Then you do not *choose* to be involved. You *are* involved. You must draw upon beliefs developed long before the crises, and turn to sources of help and strength developed long ago.

Recently, I received a phone call from a lady whom I have known for at least twenty-five years. She called to say that her mother had died. Although she and her mother had never been very close, she found herself struggling with deep feelings of guilt and regret. She was depressed, unable to function as a person, a wife, a mother. Her desperate plea was, "Teach me to grieve."

She hoped that I had a formula for casting off depression. What did I learn by watching Eva, my wife of forty-two years, die a slow death after a six-month struggle with cancer? How did I cope with these circumstances that come upon us whether we like it or not?

Her desperate phone call stimulated deep sympathy and compassion within me—but also a sense of helplessness in knowing how to respond.

Eva

Sooner or later, a crisis comes home. This happened in my home. We received news that my wife had an inoperable malignant tumor. The doctors said that unless a miracle were to happen, she had a year to live. That was November 1981. I watched her slowly lose the battle. In April 1982, she died.

Dealing with dying gives you time to think, to strengthen your grip on your present source of help, or to seek new ways to quiet the heart and mind. Eva and I had six months to prepare for her death. Forty-two years of living together had not prepared us for facing her death. But we did have time to get ready. We did not need to search for God. He was there. His Word, the Bible, was not new to us.

Eva and I faced our crisis hand in hand, one day at a time. Together we learned that we could respond to whatever comes either in a satisfied, contented manner or in a disturbed and unhappy manner. What we have been teaching these forty years stood the test in our time of trouble. We learned that, even though we entered the valley of her death together, her response to her problem depended on her beliefs. My response to her ordeal depended on my beliefs. We could review them together, but her response and mine was a personal matter. One deals with one's inner responses alone. Henry Blackaby says, "What you do next reveals what you believe about God."

We knew the promise:

> You will keep him in perfect peace, whose mind is stayed on You, because he trusts in You.
>
> Isa. 26:3

We discovered that maintaining perfect peace is quite an illusive objective. We could not keep our minds stayed on God. Our trust in Him wavered. The medical specialists offered chemical therapy and radiation as the route to healing. Eva rejected that as an option. What do you do when a medical specialist vigorously opposes her decision, when friends and associates who care object to her decision?

What do you do when you ask God for guidance and there is holy silence? We did not sleep well for several nights. We recalled a precious Bible verse:

> Let your requests be made known to God; and the peace of God, which surpasses all understanding, will guard your hearts and minds through Christ Jesus.
>
> Phil. 4:6–7

We had to face the fact that we were not peaceful. We decided the reason was because we valued the approval of the medical specialist and our friends above putting our trust in the Lord. We renewed our faith in God, and peace returned. We calmed down. The evidence of trust in God is a relaxed, cheerful, thankful spirit. We discovered that we could not, or would not, commit our minds to trust in God once and for all. Again and again we would drift away from peaceful trust in God, which had to be constantly renewed.

There was no time to consider how to handle such an event. In the twinkling of an eye, I was confronted by her death. I could turn only to resources which I was already familiar with. It is too late to seek out new ideas or unknown sources of solace in such times.

Finding a Future

Life goes on. Now I needed to discover God's wonderful plan for my life in the days ahead. I claimed a reassuring Bible verse:

> "I know the plans I have for you," declares the LORD, "plans to prosper you and not to harm you, plans to give you hope and a future. Then you will call upon me and come and pray to me, and I will listen to you. You will seek me and find me when you seek me with all your heart.
>
> Jer. 29:11–13, NIV

I looked forward happily and eagerly to the future, which is in His steady, loving hands. One thing was clear to me: I did not want to be alone. My thoughts about marriage are positive and happy. There was love, friendship, and goodwill between us. There are many reminders in my home of happy times with both Eva and Marcey, my second wife. My desire was to continue to enjoy such fellowship. I asked the Lord to send me a partner. I had been pondering Isaiah 43:18–19.

> Do not remember the former things, nor consider the things of old. Behold, I will do a new thing, now it shall spring forth; shall you not know it?

I think the verse means that we are to relinquish the past with all its happy memories and press on to embrace whatever the Lord allows in our lives.

Coping with Grief

I have come to understand more clearly that death is a part of life, and I'm comfortable with speaking of weddings and death in the same sentence. Two questions are asked me repeatedly:

• How do you handle grief?

• How do you handle coming home to an empty house?

My response to death has been shaped by my life—and how I have focused my life.

Focusing my goals. If I were to live 1,000 years, at least 920 of them would be in heaven. That is my goal—to see Jesus. "When He is revealed, we shall be like Him, for we shall see Him as He is" (1 John 3:2).

Focusing my love. The Bible tells us to love God and our neighbors (see Matt. 22:37, 39). I have tried to do that.

THE WORD FOR THE WISE

God has a big family. When death came, there was always someone there whom I loved to help me focus my love back to God.

Focusing my purpose. We are here to help others to know God. There is still much work to do. We are not here to be served, but to serve (see Mark 10:45). I have learned that if I keep my life focused properly, death becomes a normal part of life, and as our sufferings abound, "so our consolation also abounds through Christ" (2 Cor. 1:5).

Continuing Education

Here are some lessons that I have learned from coping.

1. Lasting fellowship requires a transformed heart. Human interaction ultimately exposes raw selfishness, harshness, meanness, coldness—either expressed or bottled up. We need a Savior who will "cleanse us from all unrighteousness" (1 John 1:9).

2. Lasting fellowship makes it clear that only God ultimately satisfies. Life and death go together. Some of our heroes stumble and fall. Many friends are in heaven. I have learned to be content and satisfied without any human beings around.

> You will show me the path of life; in Your presence is fullness of joy; at Your right hand are pleasures forevermore.
>
> Ps. 16:11

To sum it up, we all need a Savior and Lord who will sustain us, comfort us, quiet our hearts, and give us compassion toward others. No human being can take God's place.

Lesson: A prepared heart has no fear of death and what lies beyond.

It seems reasonable that a person who has experienced bereavement would surely be able to sympathize and empathize with another bereaved person more completely than someone who has never experienced bereavement. It follows that I should be much better able to help bereaved people than I was before experiencing the death of two wives.

Not so. My deep faith in God is not transferable. The other person must take a step of faith alone. The other person must do their own yielding. I can describe, recommend, plead, teach, and be an example. But the other person has the power of choice. If I could grasp the other person's power of choice into my possession, then I could cram the joy of the Lord and the peace of God down another person's throat whether that person likes it or not. I would force faith into their hearts.

It does not work that way. You retain your power of choice. You can eagerly embrace the biblical principles that I can share with you, or you can bitterly brush them aside.

I am learning that grieving people will respond to death and dying according to beliefs, vaguely or clearly defined, held before the crisis they now face.

People tend to concentrate on developing their outward appearance. I do not mean good grooming. I refer to the effort to make a good impression—that they are managing the ups and downs of life graciously, calmly, easily, cheerfully, and that they admire, appreciate, and accept the people who interact with them.

Comforting the Bereaved

For the Spirit-filled Christian, the inner person matches outward behavior. They fit this biblical description:

> But we all, with unveiled face, beholding as in a mirror the glory of the Lord, are being transformed into the

same image from glory to glory, just as by the Spirit of the Lord.

2 Cor. 3:18

I have had the experience of saying just the right words, keeping silent at the right time, sensing that there was something I could do. In the weeks and months that followed, the response of the bereaved indicated that my choices were most appropriate, comforting, and supporting. Their response caused me to think that I had developed some skill in dealing with the bereaved. However, I have been humbled to discover that the very same approach to another bereaved person had just the opposite effect.

My conclusion is that when you must deal with the bereaved, it is crucial to make yourself available and follow this sound biblical advice:

Trust in the LORD with all your heart, and lean not on your own understanding; in all your ways acknowledge Him, and He shall direct your paths.

Prov. 3:5–6

You will then judge your efforts by the level of your trust rather than the response of the bereaved.

Non-biblical beliefs lead you into choices that cost you peace of mind and heart. A crisis strips away a carefully constructed facade and exposes your inner person to you, though not necessarily to other people. (This is a great time to learn that in

all things God works for the good of those who love him.)

Rom. 8:28, NIV

This is a day-to-day, ever-increasing yielding of life to the Lord. One can turn away from a yielded life at any time.

It is not easily discernible how a person is handling death or what their response is to your efforts to comfort them.

When the prophet Samuel was searching for a king, the Lord said to him:

> "Do not look at his appearance or at his physical stature, because I have refused him. . . . For man looks at the outward appearance, but the LORD looks at the heart."

1 Sam. 16:7

As far as I know, human beings are not capable of "looking" at the heart.

I can give you some of my reflections based on counseling with bereaved people, interacting with bereaved people before and after the funeral, and my own personal experience with the death of people close to me (especially the death of two wives).

1. There is no way to predict how any person will react to the death of another person.

2. There is no formula that will guide you into what to say or what to do around, or for, a bereaved person. Sometimes the best thing to do is to say nothing.

Their response to death will depend on some factors that you may not know about when you attempt to comfort the bereaved. There is the relationship to the person who died and to the people who remain, the depth of the bereaved's spiritual life, and their pattern of handling multiple choices every day.

I have learned that if a person has been depending on people for strength and reassurance, that is where one will turn when death strikes. Human sympathy is wonderfully soothing in a time of need. If a person has been turning to drugs, or alcohol, or music, or a hideaway, or a car, or some other worldly source of soothing, that is where one will turn when death strikes.

If a person has a personal relationship with God, one will turn to Him when death strikes. You will drink deeply of godly comfort. God's comfort satisfies the soul. No human being or anything in this world can take the place of God's comfort. If a person has not tasted of God's comfort before this sudden death, it is quite understandable that he or she cannot know what I am talking about when thrust into a crisis. Only those who have tasted, through a close personal relationship with the Lord, can know the difference between human sympathy and God's comfort.

She Had a Secret

Mrs. Delsey illustrates a dilemma. She was glad her husband died, and she looked forward to seeing him again in heaven. However, the choices she made following his death caused her to feel like a hypocrite.

Mr. Delsey died after a long battle with cancer. He and his wife, married over forty years, had been inseparable as a couple. She hesitated to bring up what was on her mind. In a halting, almost apologetic fashion, she brought up the subject of grieving.

When the news spread that Mr. Delsey had died, there came a deluge of phone calls and visitors. Almost without exception, they expressed anxious sympathy and pity for her. They assumed that she was unhappy, miserable, disorganized, distraught. Many people warned her that the reality of death would hit her in the weeks to come.

She was at a loss as how to respond. She didn't want to disappoint these people, so she just went along with the flow and let them think that they were accurate in describing how she felt. For months, people expressed their sympathy and reassured her that her loneliness would go away with time.

She felt like a hypocrite. From the first day of Mr. Delsey's death, she was greatly relieved. The prospect of watching him struggle was over. She happily and peacefully imagined the greeting he was receiving from the Lord and the welcome prepared by many of their friends who had proceeded him.

She and her husband had explored various options open to her when the Lord called him home. They planned together what she would do. She looked forward to each day with pleasant anticipation of what the Lord had in store for her. Now, a year later, she did not experience what so many of her friends called loneliness and grieving.

Yes, she missed him, but in a contented sort of way. It was more like missing the boys when they went off to college.

She asked herself, "What is wrong with me?" She was getting along fine. It seemed strange to her that so many of her friends made Mr. Delsey's entry into the presence of the Lord the ultimate tragedy. She saw it as the supreme victory! She wanted to know how I had responded to Eva's death.

Eva and I were married for forty-two years when she died. We were surprised by the comfort and peace we received from the Lord during that time. My daughter, Sue, was with me when Eva died. Her response was, "Praise the Lord." I could not find it within myself to mourn because Eva was in heaven. True—I missed her, but in a pleasant kind of way, knowing she was with Jesus, whom we both loved and served.

Mrs. Delsy seemed relieved. It was acceptable to be contented and pleased that Mr. Delsey was in heaven. Perhaps, she mused, she should have informed her friends who came to mourn that her husband is risen and with the Lord. She repented of her hypocrisy and happily looked forward to finishing her course on earth with the Lord at her side and then to join her husband in heaven.

She did not experience grief. She was struggling with sinful behavior because she did not want to disappoint her friends.

Motorcycle Accident

I was speaking in a church, and the pastor pointed out a young lady in her early thirties who needed to talk with me.

She was a widow—the consequence of a motorcycle accident. Her husband was killed instantly. It happened two years earlier, and she continued to grieve over the loss of her husband. He was fun-loving and outgoing. She missed his friendly, cheerful presence. She always looked forward to his coming home. They were best friends. There were no children. She now lives alone in the house they were buying. She works in the church office and loves her job. When the church doors are open, she is always there. But going home is hard and lonely. Some friends have suggested that she move out of this house and live somewhere else. Her house holds too many memories.

That statement caught my attention. What kind of memories? Isn't it good to have happy memories? Is it possible that there are unhappy memories that crowd out the happy ones? I encouraged her to recall some unhappy memories toward the people who caused the accident that killed her husband.

She took me by surprise. Yes, there were unhappy memories. They centered around that motorcycle. She did not want him to buy it. In the first place, it was a strain on the budget. They could not afford a powerful motorcycle and a decent car—so they drove a ten-year-old car. They would go for long motorcycle rides in the evenings. He was a bit reckless, cutting in and out, going too fast. She hated those rides. He loved them. He insisted on riding the motorcycle to church. She despised showing up at church with her helmet and messed-up hair.

One night he proposed that they go for a ride. It was an ideal evening. She did not want to go. The discussion became heated, but she stood her ground. He went for a ride alone. A car went through a stop sign and hit him broadside. He died on the pavement.

How does she feel when she talks about this? It makes her mad. He left her with an old car, house payments, and even motorcycle payments. He was underinsured, which left her to pay off some debts. She hated writing those checks. If only he had listened to her, it would not have happened. Her thoughts were usually disapproval of his choices. She resented the position he left her in. Over and over, she would review her grudge against him.

I could see another problem. But when to speak and when to wait is often difficult to discern. The Bible says:

> Speaking the truth in love, we will in all things grow up into him who is the Head, that is, Christ.
>
> Eph. 4:15, NIV

My heart went out to her. This verse does not speak to the timing of the truth, only that it is spoken in love. This kind of interview is not the same as if she had never seen or heard of me. She had read several of my books and had heard me speak several times, so she had some idea where I was coming from.

Was she ready for my opinion? What does she think I would say? She thinks I would tell her to quit resenting her husband. But she tells herself that she is entitled to resent him. I agree. Her husband left her in a mess. She can nurse her grudge against her husband as long as she wishes. She must realize that this is happening under her skin. She is punishing herself. As long as she holds her grudge, her life is anchored in the past. For her, the past is present. Over and over again she relives the agony of that day and nurses her resentment. She can be released from this bondage anytime she is ready to let it go.

Jesus instructs us to forgive men their trespasses (see Matt. 6:14) and to love one another (see John 13:34), so I finally said, "Another option is to forgive your husband, repent of your resentment, let the Lord forgive you and then you can ask Him to fill your heart with love."

She was ready. I observed another miracle as she released her grudge, asked for forgiveness, and received the love of God in her heart. In a flash she was released from her burden, and now she is free. She can take her burden back again anytime she wants it. The decision is in her hands.

This story illustrates what happens when two problems coexist. One can overshadow the other. It seems reasonable that the tragic death of her husband would explain her misery. In this case, it was the resentment that held the sting.

The next illustration is the struggle a widow had over the loss of her family.

"Good Riddance!"

Annebel was pathetic, depressed, on the edge of tears, overwrought, sloppy. She had seen several psychologists, a psychiatrist, several pastors, and a famous evangelist. No one could help. Her condition was the result of a great tragedy, which was told to me by a friend who spoke for Annebel.

About six months before, Annebel's family was on their way to a Saturday picnic. They had forgotten the picnic basket. She stayed at the park to reserve the picnic table while her husband and two children returned home for the basket. No one knows what happened. There were no witnesses. A train struck their car at a railroad crossing and all three were killed.

Her friend described Annebel as a happily married woman, a good wife and mother who attended church regularly. Both she and her husband were Sunday School teachers. This accident obviously was a shock to the church and the community. Annebel could not seem to get over the tragedy. A normally cheerful, outgoing, active lady, she became depressed, withdrawn, and inactive.

What could I do? A long list of professionals were unable to help. I told her friend that it would be necessary for Annebel to contact me personally.

Several days went by before she called. She wanted to know if she could bring a friend along for support? That seemed a reasonable enough request. On the spot I decided that she should come alone. She refused, but I insisted. Several more days went by. She called and repeated her request. Again, I insisted on seeing her alone. She refused. I could not explain my position even to myself. She called a third time with the same request. "Why can't I bring a friend for support?" I remained firm, but this time she was willing to come alone.

The first meeting was hard. It started out with Annebel interviewing me. Had I ever experienced the death of a close family member? No. Had I ever seen anyone as a counselee who lost a family in a moment? No. I appear unsympathetic. No comment. She is not sure I could understand. I am not sure either. I can only try. There was a long silence. What could I say?

Some thoughts occurred to me. We are both Christians. I asked God for wisdom as we talked, assuming He would answer my prayer. I referred her to 2 Corinthians 1:2–5:

> Grace to you and peace from God our Father and the Lord Jesus Christ. Blessed be the God and Father of our Lord Jesus Christ, the Father of mercies and God of all comfort, who comforts us in all our tribulation, that we may be able to comfort those who are in any trouble, with the comfort with which we ourselves are comforted by God. For as the sufferings of Christ abound in us, so our consolation also abounds through Christ. Now if we are afflicted, it is for your consolation and salvation, which is effective for enduring the same sufferings which we also

suffer. Or if we are comforted, it is for your consolation and salvation.

My counsel followed this line: "We worship a God of all comfort and consolation. I presume you are here to seek these. There is something blocking or preventing your receiving comfort and consolation from God. You are receiving sympathy and attention from people, but that is not helping. We must discover what is hindering you from receiving comfort from God. Perhaps I can help you find out. It will be necessary to search your heart. You must answer all my questions. If you wish to try this approach, I'm willing to do it. Don't decide now. Go home and think and pray. Ask God to guide us. Call me if you want to continue." She called the same day, saying she is ready to search her heart.

The Real Story

Why would God not give her comfort and consolation? As I contemplated this question, I recalled a Bible verse:

> Behold, the LORD's hand is not shortened, that it cannot save; nor His ear heavy, that it cannot hear. But your iniquities have separated you from your God; and your sins have hidden His face from you, so that He will not hear.

Isa. 59:1–2

When Annebel returned, she seemed eager to begin. I told her of my thoughts and read her that Bible verse. The effect was like lancing a boil. Out tumbled this story about the day the tragedy occurred:

It was a Saturday—a beautiful sunshiny day with a gentle breeze. She thought to herself that this is a perfect day to visit her parents. It would take ninety minutes to drive there along a scenic road, one of her favorite drives. She called her mother and made arrangements to stay for supper.

Meanwhile, her husband, who worked until noon, glanced out the window and noted the same beautiful day—a perfect day for a picnic at their favorite park. Very pleased with this idea, he called his wife. She had already called her mother. He insisted on having a picnic, and told her to have the food ready when he came home. She was furious. He got busy with his work, not sensing his wife's negative response. When he came home, there was no picnic basket filled with food. They had a vicious shouting match that ended with her reluctantly calling her mother to say the visit was off. She dragged her feet in preparing food for the picnic. The children sided with their dad. They wanted a picnic in the park. He was becoming increasingly impatient with Annebel's pokiness. The more he pressed, the more rebellious she felt. Finally she was finished. He herded them into the car, and they took off—two very angry, disgusted adults. This kind of clash was nothing new. It was happening quite frequently lately.

They arrived at the park when it was discovered that no one had put the picnic basket in the car. A nasty fight followed over whose fault it was. Thoroughly disgusted, her husband decided to go after the basket. The children decided to go along. She elected to stay with the picnic table. She said, "Good riddance!" She fumed furiously while she was alone. It seemed they were gone a long time—which disgusted her more than ever.

A police car came along. They were looking for her. There had been an accident. Her husband and two children were dead. You can imagine her response. Her last words to her husband and two children were, "Good riddance!"

When she finished her story, she wept uncontrollably. I proposed that we end our session, but she wanted to continue. She hadn't shared this story with anyone until now.

Grief and Unrepented Sin

She convinced herself that she was a loving wife and mother, grieving over a beloved family. Now she had to run her story through the principles in Isaiah 59:1–2. What were her sins? I proposed that she tell me. There was a very long, tearful silence. She began to whisper: self-seeking, rebellion, anger, deception, resentment.

Did she first discover this condition the day of the accident? No, this was a problem before she met her husband. She had become skilled at justifying such behavior, or blaming it on someone else. I thought of 1 Corinthians 15:56:

The sting of death is sin, and the strength of sin is the law.

The combination of these tragic deaths and weighing her behavior on the scales of the law seemed to say to us that there is no denying the truth. In the presence of death, our sins sting us and weigh heavily on our hearts.

Are there verses telling us that her grieving is not the result of this tragedy? Rather, is her grieving the consequence of the unrepented sin? I think so. What does Annebel think? She thinks so too. If it's sin, there is no human remedy. Only God can help. Repentance is the key. Repentance implies that I am wrong and sorry and willing to be cleansed and renewed. Is she willing? She buried her face in her hands and tearfully cried out to God. It was a holy scene. When she finished and looked up, she didn't look like the same person. She claimed that she was at ease for the first time in many years.

Before our meeting, she thought that admitting her condition would flood her with guilt. But now she feels washed and clean and relieved. It was the other way around. Ignoring her sins produced misery and guilt. She was indeed a new person. Now she was free to yield to the Holy Spirit. Her friends marveled at the change. What a miracle!

◆

10

Adultery

Sex is the most popular subject there is. Everyone enjoys the ecstasy of physical contact, the subtle pleasure of skin against skin.

There is first of all the subtle pleasure of simply looking and enjoying the beauty of the human body, whether you are looking at a painting, a photograph, or a live body. Looking can quickly change from healthy, wholesome admiration and appreciation for the body to lust.

Lust is a handy and pleasurable sin. The whole body can be lustfully quickened as you look and sound like an angel. You can develop the art of lusting without letting on that you even noticed anything stimulating.

The whole field of pornography is based on the lust of the eyes that quickens the whole body. The way we dress is often with the lust of the eye in mind. Jesus said,

> "You have heard that it was said to those of old, 'You shall not commit adultery. . . .' But I say to you that whoever looks at a woman to lust for her has already committed adultery with her in his heart."
>
> Matt. 5:27–28

Jesus stood on solid ground when they brought Him a woman caught in the act of adultery. He invited anyone who was without sin to cast the first stone. Everyone left.

Then there is the pleasure of skin against skin. Touching can stimulate the body in a pleasurable sensation. Touching leads to fondling, which can pleasantly electrify the body. When two people go much beyond touching, reason is short-circuited and the desire to complete the sex act is all that matters. Such behavior takes place in a moment of ecstatic pleasure, and then the participants spend years picking up the pieces.

Adultery is a terrible thing. Anybody that I counsel with knows very well what I think of adultery. Anybody who is committing adultery is sinning against God and flirting with hell. But the biblical counselor can say it lovingly, tenderly, and kindly. Jesus did. You almost think He was inconsistent, would you not? We talk about the wrath of God. Then we talk about Jesus' taking the side of the adulteress. However, he did *not* approve of her adultery.

Obviously adultery is an act of the sinful nature. The counselee tends to be preoccupied with the act of adultery. My objective is to find out *what else is wrong in the life.* If we do not deal with the rest of the awfulness in the heart, the counselee is a good candidate for repeating it anyway. So let us find out what is in the heart and get it all out on the table. The Lord will cleanse and heal and forgive.

When He has cleansed and healed and forgiven, that is it. You are as white as snow.

Adultery and Other Sins

I have found that adultery is accompanied by other acts of the sinful nature as well. Hatred is just as sinful as adultery. The final act of adultery is the last in a series of fights and strife and nastiness and bitterness. I am just as sympathetic with the adulterer as the other party. Here is a list of some sins that are associated with adultery:

- debauchery
- hatred
- discord
- jealousy

- fits of rage
- selfish ambition
- dissensions

When adultery is involved, some of these are also present in both marriage partners.

I have learned to turn a problem into a teaching situation and instruct people in the works of the flesh. Mutual misery is a powerful magnetic attraction which sometimes results in adultery.

Let this be clear. I am not proposing that we minimize the seriousness of adultery. I am saying that we must teach that the rest of the acts of the sinful nature are just as serious as adultery.

Question: How would you counsel a person who came to you and admits they are having an adulterous affair? What about telling his or her partner?

Answer: If the counselee is uncertain about telling it, I would advise to keep quiet until that person has a burden—a clear-cut burden. This must be communicated to the partner, but when there are doubts, do not.

Putting the Pieces Back Together

What will happen when the other partner finds out? That all depends on the spiritual condition of the partner, not on the behavior of the adulterer.

What if the partner responds in anger, rebellion, and unforgiveness? He or she can be cleansed. This is the good news! Jesus came into the world to give us power over our own sins. An unforgiving spirit is not caused by another person's choices. It is *revealed* by another's choice.

In case of adultery, what if the offended partner will not forgive? We cannot make anyone forgive. The counselee waits, prays for the partner, and stays out of the way. The person prays for the grace and patience to endure hardship until the offended partner repents. The unforgiving spirit is something we cannot change in others. After all, nobody can make anybody else repent of their sin. Remember, unforgiveness is sin.

Question: There are sex clinics and sex therapists. Some married people are going to sex lectures thinking the lectures can resolve their problem and heal their marriages. I am sure you have had many couples come with this kind of a problem. How do you treat that?

Answer: Very few people during their courting days had any problem. Only after marriage do they say they have a sex problem.

It is not a sex problem: it is a symptom. The most ecstatic, pleasurable experience in the world is to have sexual relations. No one would dispute that. Do you remember when you were single and you wanted to kiss a girl? You figured out how, one way or another. When you dated, the problem was not whether you liked physical contact; the problem was restraint. Is it not incredible that six months later, they walk in and say, "I cannot stand this person to touch me"? This is the same person they could not wait to get touched by! This physical drive is so strong, they will figure out a technique. Sex problems have nothing to do with technique. Sex problems have nothing to do with attraction.

When you discover someone who is having difficulty with physical expression, it is like alcoholism. You look elsewhere for the problem. What you will find is that a man and his wife have accumulated a whole bunch of unresolved issues—deadlocks. He is doing things she does not like, and he refuses to quit.

Newlyweds came to see me. He has not touched her in two weeks. They quibble over neatness. He does not hang up his coat. Her cooking is terrible. He grumbles. Then he wants her to jump in his arms!

What should he do? Hang up his coat. Learn to eat her food. They do not have a sexual problem. Perhaps sexual therapy solved their problem for the moment, but the counselor was appealing to selfishness. The husband wanted something bad enough to hang up his coat. Now she was getting her own way.

I had to tell them it was only a temporary solution. Unless they dealt with their selfishness, they would be back. They came out of sexual frustration (that is what they called it), but what caused it? Self-centeredness.

Flattery

I am now counseling with a young woman who has committed adultery. A young man told her she was a gorgeous, irresistible person. She loved being around him. They got more and more involved and committed adultery. But she could not help it. He would not let her alone. What is the truth? She was subject to flattery and she liked it. He was not irresistible. Her morals simply collapsed around him.

The backdrop for this problem is a heart crammed full of bitterness and hate toward an inconsiderate husband.

I am counseling another person who has committed adultery. She has told me she was forced into it. She struggled against it but could not help but yield. It is not true. No matter what she says about herself, the only way that can happen is if she cooperated. Do not kid yourself; adultery begins in the heart. Do you have that conviction? It is important that you do.

Where does hope come from? People come to me and say that they are caught in a web. They have a feeling of hopelessness; everything is gone. All they need to do is turn to the source of hope: God. He will lead them out of this. He will put them on their feet and give them a ministry. "After what I have done?" Yes, after what you have done. "How can I ever be happy again?" By turning to the source of joy. Very simple.

Physical Attraction vs. Commitment

Problem: A couple got married but now feel they never loved each other, and had rather be single again.

Solution: What couple has not! Marriage is not the answer. How do you demonstrate love? Would you kiss? We confuse physical response with love. Sexuality and love are not the same thing.

Do you lose your eyesight or normal physical attraction to other people just because you're married? What are we talking about then? (Some will say, "If you love me, you will buy this or that, or let me go out with the boys." What do you do to prove your love? A kiss can be as phony as it can be real.)

The physical attraction you have toward your wife is the same as you had for other women before you married.

But in marriage you have a *special* relationship. Marriage is a commitment. Love is a work of the Spirit. You may have been physically attracted to your partner and called that love.

Nobody is disinterested in sex. You can go into any library and look at the edge of a book that has a chapter on sex, and it will be the most worn from use! But conflict between you and your spouse is what makes touching that individual undesirable, whereas before it was highly desirable.

When we talk about losing our love, we mean we are building an invisible wall of unresolved reactions toward your partner. Take that wall down and what is it made of? Wrath, anger, bitterness, stubbornness, resentment, jealousy, and envy. You deal with those, and you will find your sexual response being restored toward our partner.

The Spectrum of Love

Something that Henry Drummond wrote in the last century may help you see how we are to love. In a booklet titled *The Greatest Thing in the World*, he referred to love as described by Paul in 1 Corinthians 13 and likened it to light. If you pass light through a crystal prism, it emerges on the other side of the prism broken into its component parts: every color of the rainbow. The apostle Paul passes love through the prism of his inspired intellect and it comes out on the other side broken into its elements. Drummond calls this the Spectrum of Love. It has nine components:

1. Patience	"Love suffers long
2. Kindness	and is kind;
3. Generosity	love does not envy;
4. Humility	love does not parade itself, is not puffed up;
5. Courtesy	does not behave rudely,

6. Unselfishness	does not seek its own,
7. Good temper	is not provoked,
8. Guilelessness	thinks no evil;
9. Sincerity	does not rejoice in iniquity, but rejoices in the truth."

Study of the Spectrum of Love will lead you to understand that as you demonstrate your love for God, you will be loving your marriage partner and your family—and, indeed, everybody—in the same love. You will not be loving God and your partner also, as if they were two separately directed loves. You will not love others as if this were a third love. Rather, you will love your partner and others all within the framework of loving God and letting His love flow through you.

Paul leaves no doubt about the source of such love.

May the Lord make your love increase and overflow for each other and for everyone else, just as ours does for you.

1 Thess. 3:12, NIV

The apostle John adds,

Beloved, let us love one another, for love is of God; and everyone who loves is born of God and knows God.

1 John 4:7

Since God is the source, this love can be universally applied. It is spiritual fruit. It is to know no limits. It is broader than the union of two people in a marriage. Thus, it cannot be love that sets a man and woman apart as a special, united flesh.

The Marriage Relationship

If it is not love that produces the uniqueness of marriage, what is it? It is the relationship—the duties and details of marriage—that sets a man and a woman apart.

All of us are involved in a number of relationships. Some unite us with fellow workers in a job, with neighbors in a community undertaking, with other Christians in the conduct of a local church program. Each relationship has its own peculiarities, its own limits. Marriage is the most sacred and intimate of all relationships. But if love is a universal thing, marriage has no monopoly on it.

Does this mean you are to love your neighbor's wife as you do your own wife? The Spectrum of Love says yes. Does this give thoughts of or lead to an illicit relationship? Of course not. You have the answer in the word *relationship*. Love never got anyone into trouble. Relationships often do. You are to love all people. The relationship that binds you and your mate together is exclusively yours.

The relationship of marriage, however, is not a guarantor of happiness. A husband and wife may live under the same roof, spend each other's money, sleep in the same room, eat together, give birth to children from a shared physical experience. But without the undergirding of God's love, the intimacies of the marriage relationship can drive a couple apart.

To yield to the love of God is to produce a perfect love toward others, including the marriage partner. Conversely, faulty relationships result from a faulty relationship with God. A marriage based on sincere love for God can be disturbed only when something comes between one or the other of the individuals and God.

Once again, look at this Scripture:

> May the Lord make your love increase and overflow for each other and for everyone else, just as ours does for you.
>
> 1 Thess. 3:12, NIV

If this is true, my love should grow toward everyone. How is it that I can love my wife, your wife, and you? Read 1 Corinthians 13—it is that kind of love that will hold your marriage together.

How do you show love? It is something you are, not something you do. You do something in a spirit of kindness, and I can duplicate it in a spirit of hate. Love involves a relationship between you and God and does not have anything to do with your partner. If you say you have lost your love for your partner, you are saying you have drifted away from an effective relationship with God. The presence of your partner makes it obvious.

I am trying to point out that marriage is a relationship, a commitment—a special kind of relationship, but not a special kind of emotion.

Why are marriages collapsing all over the world? Because we are looking for some kind of chemistry that does not exist.

◆

11

How to Deal with Anger

If I were forced to rank a list of sins from the worst to the least destructive, I would have a problem in ranking number one and number two. After fifty years of working with troubled people, the top two sins would be anger and deceit. I would rank them above stealing, fornication, adultery, and murder.

This chapter is condensed from chapters in *When You're Tired of Treating the Symptoms and You're Ready for a Cure [The Heart of the Problem]*, and *Breaking Free from the Bondage of Sin*.

The *American Heritage Dictionary* defines anger this way:

an•ger *n.* 1. A feeling of extreme displeasure, hostility, indignation, or exasperation toward someone or something; rage; wrath; ire. 2. OBSOLETE. Trouble; pain;

THE WORD FOR THE WISE

affliction. Synonyms: anger, rage, fury, ire, wrath, resentment, indignation.

These nouns denote varying degrees of marked displeasure. Anger, the most general, denotes strong, usually temporary displeasure without specifying manner of expression. Rage and fury are closely related in the sense of intense, uncontained, explosive emotion. Fury can be more destructive, rage more justified by circumstances. Ire is a poetic term for anger. Wrath applies especially to fervid anger that seeks vengeance or punishment on an epic scale. Resentment refers to ill will and suppressed anger generated by a sense of grievance. One feels indignation at seeing the mistreatment of someone or something dear and worthy.[1]

The Universality of Anger

Not everyone is an alcoholic; not everyone steals, or swears, or commits adultery. But *everyone struggles with anger*. It is a universal problem. I have observed it among primitive cannibals in Irian Jaya, among illiterate people in tiny villages deep in the forest of Zaire, among my playmates when I was a child, in my parents, in church members, in pastors, in highly educated people, in the very rich, in people in government. And yes, in me.

You cannot decide to be angry. You can take elaborate precautions to avoid being angry. But, sooner or later, anger underneath your skin is triggered by memory, someone's behavior, a conversation, a phone call, or a letter. It can cause your heart to beat faster, make you sweat, tense up your muscles, foul up your digestive system, alter the way you think, dictate how you act, and trigger words from your mouth.

There seems to be universal agreement that anger must be tamed. Yet there is vast disagreement over the cause and the cure.

A memorable time that I was conscious that I could not manage my anger occurred in my late twenties. At that time, I had a boss that kept me riled up most of the day, a wife who persisted in frustrating me by doing things her way rather than my way, and a toddler who irritated me by simply wanting my attention when I didn't want to give it. These three people backed me into a corner. They didn't even know it. They forced me to face up to the fact that there was something in me that was activated by them and turned me into a person who said things I was sorry for, did things that I regretted, thought things that frightened me, and caused my body (heart, stomach, muscles) to malfunction.

The solution came for me when I was convinced that I was helpless and needed to be saved from myself. The Bible describes my condition exactly:

> Now if I do what I do not want to do, it is no longer I who do it, but it is sin living in me that does it.
>
> Rom. 7:20

Clearly the law of sin was controlling my body.

A Faulty Perception of Anger

This sentence sums up what almost everyone declares who comes to the consulting room with an anger problem: "My anger is a normal and justifiable response to the way I was treated."

Seldom does one inquire about the possibility of anger being sin in their hearts. That word has almost disappeared from their vocabulary. Instead, people declare that they are unhappy, tense, anxious, worried, disappointed, misunderstood, mistrusted, unloved, or under extreme pressure. The buzz words are *stressed out* or *burned out*.

Frequently I listen to highly intelligent, competent, educated, successful people say the strangest things, such as:

- "I blew up," or "I exploded." People say this very sincerely. Of course this never happens. Picture a person blowing up: teeth, bones, eyeballs, arms, legs, body parts flying in all directions.

- "I broke down." Can you see this quivering, helpless body collapsed in a heap?

- "I lost my head." Can you picture such an unlikely sight of a headless person groping around?

- "She gets under my skin." One can accept the presence of a microscopic creature having entered the body, but hardly a full-grown woman.

- "My blood was boiling." This person is no doubt experiencing some bodily changes, but hardly the condition described here.

- "I was beside myself." This statement simply defies logic.

- "He turns me on."

- "He turns me off."

- "He burns me up."

- "I am fed up."

My purpose in recording these statements is not to belittle anyone or to treat their reports lightly. These are socially acceptable terms describing bodily changes that we are aware of as we interact with people and respond to the events of the day.

We freely describe ourselves and our problems as being caused by other people. But it is very difficult to say the simple words, "I am wrong. I have sinned."

A Personal Encounter with Anger

Recently my wife and I were on our way to lecture about anger. We went out to rent a car for the trip. I was seated beside the desk of the person who had to fill out the car-rental form.

Just as we began filling out the form, his phone rang and he talked with a customer about car-rental information. Several more times as we filled out the form the phone rang. I became nervous and looked at my watch. Twenty-five minutes had passed.

Finally I said, "Will you let someone else answer the phone or get someone else to fill out this form!"

Just then my wife walked into the office and overheard my statement. She asked, "What are you upset about?"

"I'm not upset," I shot back, "I'm just trying to get this form filled out."

"You are not being very nice to that poor fellow. Can't you see how busy he is?" she scolded.

"I've been sitting here twenty-five minutes," I tried to explain.

Finally we were on our way. There was a brittle silence between us. I felt quite righteous about being ignored by that agent and being misunderstood by my wife.

About half an hour later my cold shoulder toward my wife began to thaw. At last, I could admit that I was angry at that agent and my wife. Neither one of them caused it; their behavior revealed my anger.

When I became aware of my wrongdoing, I realized that if I continued on in that anger and did not repent on the spot it would clearly be sinful. I did repent, and fellowship with my wife was restored and my response to the rental agent was forgiven.

I believe that Ephesians 4:26 is saying that when you are aware of an unloving response to anyone, you should repent immediately. If there is no repentance, it could lead to other acts of the sinful nature.

You would think that everyone would leap at the chance to be rid of sin. Not so. Usually, people do not seek a real cure to their problems (sins); they just want relief from the consequences of their sins.

I'm not some stranger to this material. I'm the one that is teaching and practicing it. But between conferences, look what happened. I don't always know why it happens, but when it does I need to call it by its right name: sin. In my case, I not only blew up at my wife, but I also tried to tell her she was wrong!

Anger Is Destructive

Negative responses can cause much misery in life. Edward Strecker and Kenneth Appel have compiled a list of words that people use to describe anger:

> When the presence of anger is detected in a person, we say he is mad, bitter, frustrated, griped, fed up, sore, hot under the collar, excited (now don't get excited), seething, annoyed, troubled, inflamed, indignant, antagonistic, exasperated, vexed, furious, provoked, hurt, irked, sick (she makes me sick), pained (he gives me a pain), cross, hostile, ferocious, savage, vicious, deadly, dangerous, offensive.

Then, since anger is energy and impels individuals to do things intending to hurt or destroy, there is a whole series of verbs which depict actions motivated by anger: to hate, wound, damage, annihilate, despise, scorn, disdain, loathe, vilify, curse, despoil, ruin, demolish, abhor, abominate, desolate, ridicule, tease, kid, get even, laugh at, humiliate, goad, shame, criticize, cut, take out spite on, rail at, scold, bawl out, humble, irritate, beat up, take for a ride, ostracize, fight, beat, vanquish, compete with, brutalize, curse, offend, bully.[2]

It is my observation that almost everyone resists calling any kind of anger sin. Multitudes of people (including me) have faced up to problems such as drinking, swearing, or stealing as sin and it's behind us. It's been dealt with.

Dealing with anger is different. You can be completely and totally repentant over your anger. Confession leads to welcome relief from tension. I suspect that most people experience some anger every week. You think you have dealt with it, and it shows up again.

I have observed that one difficulty in dealing with anger is the wide range of intensity with which it can be expressed. On the one end there is such extreme anger that it leads to violent physical abuse or even murder. We have no difficulty recognizing such anger as sin. But on the other end of the continuum is anger that is so mild as to be almost unnoticeable. This "annoyance level" of anger is easy to ignore; for example, mild frustration at a child who won't make his bed; at a nearly empty gas tank in the car; at a traffic light; or at an impolite clerk.

You can compare anger to the flow of contaminated water in a tub. A wide open faucet yields the same kind of water as a dripping faucet. One drip at a time will gradually fill a tub if the drain hole is plugged. It may take weeks to fill the tub with contaminated water, but eventually one more drop will make the water spill over the top. All that water came from the same polluted source.

Extreme anger is easy to recognize and impossible to ignore. The body pumps adrenaline into the bloodstream causing the heartbeat to accelerate, the blood pressure to rise, the mouth to become dry, the muscles to become tense, the mental faculties to become alert, and the emotions to become disturbed.

Adrop of anger is not so easy to recognize. To put it another way, it is easy to ignore. Bodily changes are hardly noticeable, but the effects are cumulative. The symptoms are anxiety, restlessness, tension. Drops of anger build up in the body. Finally, one more incident (major or minor), and anger spills over the top. I listen to people who are puzzled over responses that surprise themselves:

"I heard myself screaming at the children to come into the house."

"I was so mad, I actually hit her. It was over which tie to wear."

"Even though he lives a thousand miles away, at times when someone mentions his name, I am fully consumed with anger in a matter of seconds."

Effects of Anger Can Build Up Slowly

Wayne Hartley was an angry man. He moved from job to job because "worldly people" irked him. Finally he landed at a firm with a Christian president. Here was a man he felt he could work for; he looked forward to a happy relationship on the job.

But things did not turn out that way. Hartley was made a general manager, having a number of foremen to supervise. One of the foremen used a great deal of profanity. One day Hartley could stand his talk no longer, so he called the foreman aside and ordered him to refrain. The foreman paid no attention, so Hartley warned him again, "Stop it, or you'll get fired!"

The company president heard about Hartley's ultimatum. He called in his general manager. "Joe has a foul mouth, I know," the president said. "But he gets more work out of his crew than any of our other foremen."

He told Hartley to leave the foreman alone. Hartley was not to impose his private standards on Joe or any other employee. Reluctantly Hartley accepted the president's directive. But from that day on he felt he was constantly being overruled by the president. One day when he heard the foreman curse, it was the drop that spilled over the top. He stormed into the president's office, demanding a showdown.

"Am I the general manager or not?" he thundered.

"Why do you ask? Do you think you are the president?"

Wayne Hartley saw red. He shouted at his superior, waving his finger under the boss' nose. He was angry from the top of his head to the soles of his feet.

Telling of the incident later, Wayne said: "It takes a lot to get me mad, but when I am, the fur really flies. There we stood, toe-to-toe and nose-to-nose, yelling at each other. And both of us profess to be Christians. But you can be sure of this: No non-Christian ever made me more miserable than that man."

Did the company president cause Wayne Hartley to blow up?

"Who else?" Wayne demanded. "The last time he crossed me was the very last straw. I don't lose control of myself unless I'm forced to."

In looking back over his life, Wayne could see that he had possessed an antagonistic spirit since childhood. It had come out at home, at school, toward his wife, and his children, toward anyone who thwarted him. He did not blow up very often, but when he did, everyone got out of his way. He controlled things pretty well by simply threatening to blow up. At times, however, he met persons who just let him blow. This was true of the people he worked with; and this explained why he moved from job to job. By such moves he was able to dismiss his own problem, saying that his reasons for moving were the worldliness, selfishness, or cantankerousness of others. He always had a good reason for his tantrums.

What was Wayne Hartley doing? He was accumulating wrath day after day. And he even denied that he himself had anything to do with it. His situation could be likened to the tub with a dripping faucet. Put the plug in and the tub fills up. The next drop will cause the water to run over. Is it the last drop that spills the water onto the floor? No, it's the last drop plus all the rest of the drops. Similarly the last drop, or "the last straw," would cause Wayne to blow up.

> And God is able to make all grace abound toward you, that you, always having all sufficiency in all things, may have an abundance for every good work.
>
> 2 Cor. 9:8

Could such grace be available to Wayne Hartley? Yes. First, however, he had to take an honest look at himself. When he did, he saw that he brought a spirit of antagonism to his new job. He didn't like to be crossed—whether by the foreman who violated his standard of speech or by the president who refused to let him impose his standard on another. The frustration of not getting his own way exposed the wrath within him.

When Wayne accepted the fact that the foreman's cursing triggered the wrath that was already in him, he could see that it was sin. You don't deal with your own sin by ordering someone else to stop cursing. You must go to God. He will cleanse you of your sin if you reach out for His help. He will give you a tender, compassionate heart toward the poor man who finds a crumb of relief by cursing.

And that is the good news for everyone filled with anger and malice and bitterness. The people in your life may never change their ways. Circumstances may be beyond your control. But fortunately you can do something about yourself. You can open your heart to God, who is able to fill it with bountiful grace. But whether you allow God to give you His grace is your decision.

Our response to people and circumstances on the outside of us constantly reminds us of the condition inside us: an imperfect spiritual life which seems easier to justify or deny than to face.

What the Bible Says about Anger

Most persons who seek counsel will argue that they have the right to be angry. "Under my circumstances, can you blame me?" they will say in stout defense. Of course they have the *right* to be angry. But as long as they argue in defense of their wrath, they will see no need nor have any desire to change and thus be delivered from the unhappiness of anger.

One of the most quoted verses in the Bible is this one:

Be angry and do not sin: do not let the sun go down on your wrath

Eph. 4:26

My counselees uniformly declare that this verse means that their kind of anger is not sin. However, there is a part of that verse that is not debatable: Call your anger righteous if you will, but get rid of it by sundown.

Just five verses down from the "Be angry and sin not" verse, it clearly states that we can let anger be put away from us (see Eph. 4:31). Galatians 5:16 says clearly that people who walk in the Spirit need not struggle with anger, which is an act of the sinful nature. There is no human remedy. Only God can cleanse your heart.

Notice what other biblical advice there is about the management of anger:

For the wrath of man does not produce the righteousness of God.

James 1:20

Do not take revenge, my friends, but leave room for God's wrath, for it is written: "It is mine to avenge; I will repay," says the Lord.

Rom. 12:19, NIV

Let all bitterness, wrath, anger, clamor, and evil speaking be put away from you, with all malice.

Eph. 4:31

Cease from anger, and fosake wrath; do not fret—it only causes harm.

Ps. 37:8

Do not hasten in your spirit to be angry, for anger rests in the bosom of fools.

Eccl. 7:8

It seems clear to me that the Bible is telling us that God expects us to tackle the problems around us with His love in our hearts. Read on:

"But I say to you, love your enemies . . . and pray for those who spitefully use you and persecute you."

Matt. 5:44

Husbands, love your wives.

Eph. 5:25

Admonish the younger women to love their husbands, to love their children.

Titus 2:4

"'You shall love your neighbor as yourself.'"

Matt. 22:39

Love the brotherhood of believers.

1 Pet. 2:17, NIV

May the Lord make your love increase and overflow for each other and for everyone else.

1 Thess. 3:12, NIV

Now hope does not disappoint, because the love of God has been poured out in our hearts by the Holy Spirit who was given to us.

Rom. 5:5

Who shall separate us from the love of Christ? Shall tribulation, or distress, or persecution, or famine, or nakedness, or peril, or sword? For I am persuaded that neither death nor life, nor angels nor principalities nor poers, nor things present nor things to come, nor height nor depth, nor any other created thing, shall be able to separate us from the love for God which is in Christ Jesus our Lord.

Rom. 8:35, 38–39

Jesus' response to evildoers, as they crucified Him between two criminals, was:

"Father, forgive them, for they do not know what they do."

Luke 23:34

But the difficult problem is how can a human being who naturally responds angrily to the circumstances of life, change from responding in anger to responding in love? Humanly speaking, we must admit that this biblical advice is impossible to attain. We all know that to bottle up or swallow anger is not the solution. Bottled up anger can ruin your health and twist your thinking. You would become like a walking time bomb, set to explode at some external provocation.

The Bible offers a radical solution: "Put it away. Stop it." This is humanly impossible. Yes, it takes a miracle. You need supernatural help.

The Steps to Change

Step 1: Recognize Anger as Sin

The biblical prescription for dealing with destructive anger is precise and strong. Strife, malice, hatred, anger, outbursts of wrath, dissension, and contention are works of the flesh—of the sinful nature (see Gal. 5:19–21; Col. 3:8). They are sin, and that's good news, because there is a divine solution for sin. God promises to help you. Dealing with sin is His specialty.

> Salvation is found in no one else, for there is no other name under heaven given to men by which we must be saved.
>
> Acts 4:12, NIV

A simple step that gives you a source of strength to "stop" angry responses is to invite Jesus to come into your life. Yet many competent, able people have a hard time accepting the fact that they need supernatural help.

"I can manage my anger. Isn't that good enough?" It certainly beats exploding. However, only God can help you to stop it. Because anger is sin, you need a Savior who will cleanse you of your sins.

> If we confess our sins, He is faithful and just to forgive us our sins and to cleanse us from all unrighteousness.
>
> 1 John 1:9

Step 2: Replace Anger with Godly Emotions

When you have a forgiven, cleansed heart, you can ask God for the power of the Holy Spirit to produce the fruit of the Spirit in your life (see Gal. 5:22–23):

- love
- joy
- goodness
- faithfulness

- peace
- long-suffering
- kindness
- gentleness
- self-control

You will still have problems, face injustices, and encounter difficult people—as everyone does. You will still need to be energized, alerted, and motivated to correct what needs correcting. But a Christian knows that a person energized by the Holy Spirit with love, joy, peace, long-suffering, kindness, goodness, faithfulness, gentleness, and self-control has the strength to conquer the bitter, sarcastic words; anxiety; bodily tensions; and violent behavior that formerly characterized him.

The apostle Paul says it best:

> So I say, live by the Spirit, and you will not gratify the desires of the sinful nature.
>
> Gal. 5:16, NIV

A Christian does not always surrender to God perfectly anymore than he can manage himself perfectly. Few people make it through any given day perfectly. But you can catch anger at the earliest possible point.

The Bible says these virtues are from a source out of this world. God controls an infinite supply. Virtues will flow through the one who is cleansed from sin as his body is yielded to the Spirit of God. The result is access to a supernatural resource that a person can draw upon.

Drawing upon God can be compared to drawing water. When you open a faucet, water flows out. Water is made up of two parts: hydrogen (a gas) and oxygen (also a gas). These invisible units combine into a product called water. A glassful will quench your thirst. You can fill a tub and take a bath in it. You can irrigate a thousand-acre farm with it. You can use all you want because you are drawing from a reservoir of water. All you need to do is to keep the pipes in good repair and open the faucet. The water will flow. Amazingly, you can stop the flow of a massive reservoir of water by simply closing the faucet.

In similar fashion, when you allow Jesus to come into your body as your Savior, not only are you cleansed from your sin, but you also have access to the Spirit of God. Here is an invisible, unexplainable presence that produces visible, measurable changes in the way your body works. Your body is transformed.

Phillip Keller describes this miracle:

> deceivers become honest; the vile become noble; the vicious become gentle; the selfish become selfless; the hard-hearted become affectionate; the weak become strong. Once a person is yielded to the Holy Spirit, there can be no pretending to be pleasant and pious while within one seethes and boils with pent-up perversions. Apart from the Spirit of God in control, other human beings' ill will, hatred, bitterness, envy, old grudges, jealousy and other heinous attitudes can be masked with a casual shrug or forced half smile.[3]

Nothing in *this world* can cause a person to change so radically. No longer do circumstances or people determine the condition under your skin. You can now respond to the troublesome people in your life with unconditional love, joy, peace, long-suffering, kindness, goodness, faithfulness, gentleness, and self-control. By yielding to the Spirit of God, an infinite, endless supply flows through you. There is enough for a minor irritation or a major tragedy.

Personal Loss

I watched the life of my wife of forty-two years slowly ebb away, was diagnosed with Parkinson's disease, and lost more than $250,000 in business in the same time period. There was enough peace, joy, and comfort to draw upon for each day while all three events were happening. Yet the will to draw upon the supply must come from me. No other human being or event can stop this from happening to me. However, I can, by an act of my will, cease to yield and stop the flow of this infinite supply in my body.

When my wife was ill with a fatal cancer, she learned a lesson and taught it to me. You can be sick and sinful. She cautioned us not to jump to the conclusion that emotional reactions while you are sick are caused by being sick.

One example will suffice. When she told me this story, she was enduring a lot of pain. But her eyes sparkled and she seemed pleased as though she had received a pearl of great price. Eva's pride and joy was her kitchen. At this stage of her illness she was bedridden and could no longer work in the kitchen. Many friends came to help. She could hear them in her kitchen. She would nurse waves of anger and resentment because she couldn't control her kitchen. It didn't matter that she never verbalized her feelings; her attitude was unacceptable in God's presence.

She was not sure how it happened. As she lay there it became clear to her that she was nursing a sinful heart. It was as though someone offered to clean it up by removing the bad attitudes and replacing them with gratitude and joy. She thought it was the Lord. She had a choice: She could keep her sinful heart, or choose cleansing and joy. She chose the latter.

Her last month on this earth was a time when she was so appreciative and content it seemed unreal. It was!

I am mystified that anyone would turn his back on the invitation to find rest because he refuses to take a step of faith. God's Word gives a perfect solution:

A heart at peace gives life to the body, but envy rots the bones.

Prov. 14:30

When you realize you have sinned, take it to God. The apostle John says it well:

My little children, these things I write to you, so that you may not sin. And if anyone sins, we have an Advocate with the Father, Jesus Christ the righteous. And he Himself is the propitiation for our sins, and not for ours only but also for the whole world.

1 John 2:1–2

Ponder these verses:

"First cleanse the inside of the cup and dish, that the outside of them may be clean also."

Matt. 23:26

"God is Spirit, and those who worship Him must worship in spirit and truth."

John 4:24

I say then: Walk in the Spirit, and you shall not fulfill the lust of the flesh.

Gal. 5:16

But the wisdom that comes from heaven is first of all pure; then peace-loving, considerate, submissive, full of mercy and good fruit, impartial and sincere.

James 3:17, NIV

Now hope does not disappoint, because the love of God has been poured out in our hearts by the Holy Spirit who was given to us.

Rom. 5:5

Replacing Anger with Love

A Belligerent Father

Conversations can sometimes take unexpected directions.

A calm, quiet-appearing man asked me some questions about his prayer life.

He said, "I make promises to the Lord and ask Him for the help to carry them out, but I always fail. Then I feel let down by God, and that makes me feel guilty."

"What have you asked God to help you do?" I asked.

"I promised the Lord that I would get up at 5:30 every morning and spend an hour in devotions; but I am so sleepy I can't concentrate," he answered.

"Why do you want to get up at 5:30 a.m. for devotions?"

This question triggered the reason he came to see me. He had a quick temper. I discovered that a casual conversation with his wife, which didn't go his way, could suddenly turn him into an angry, shouting person who would say mean, cutting words.

He would punish his children severely over simple mistakes. In one instance, when one of his children reached across the table for a piece of bread instead of asking someone to pass it to her, in a flash of anger he hit her so hard that he knocked her off the chair. Another time he caught his son in the garage, a place known as "off-limits" to the children. The father hit his son so hard that he left a bruise.

Thus, he thought it would help if he got up at 5:30 in the morning for devotions.

This man was trying to do penance for his anger. Jesus already died to atone for his sins. He needed to repent of his bitter, hostile spirit and ask the Lord to forgive and cleanse him and empower him to love his family.

That was a hard pill for him to swallow. It took him a while to give up his favorite reason for his temper. He liked the idea that "he was born that way" so he didn't have to claim responsibility for his temper. He decided to see what would happen if, by faith, he acknowledged his temper to be his responsibility. He asked the Lord for forgiveness and cleansing and strength. Now, he rejoices in his new relationship to the Lord. He is clean, washed, and has a new source of peace and love.

An Unfaithful Husband

A certain couple came to visit me. The wife sat there seething with animosity toward her husband. She had just learned that he was unfaithful to her throughout their thirty-year marriage. Dozens of other women were involved. Her husband sat there looking contrite. He had a long history of deception, hypocrisy, and satisfying his lusts.

He claimed to be genuinely repentant. No one would believe him. They said he was only sorry he got caught. He said his wife, who was normally a pleasant person, had become an angry, hateful, unresponsive person. She said it was his fault. He did not know what more he could do. He wanted to know if I believed him.

My answer? "God loves both of you enough to have sacrificed His Son for your sins and to give you access to the fruit of the Spirit. I love both of you, too, but I have no way of knowing the condition of your hearts."

The good news is that her husband's behavior could not come between her and God. She could call on God at any time and exchange her animosity for love, joy, peace, and kindness. All were available for the asking. She would still need to deal with her marital problem—even after a change of heart.

Her husband had the same access to God. He could exchange his sins for the fruit of the Spirit.

I have seen others dealing with sin also:

- A woman unfaithful to her husband
- A man who beat his wife's face into a black-and-blue mess
- A couple who swindled widows of tens of thousands of dollars
- A teenage thief
- A man tormented by the memory of raping and killing a woman
- A woman who walked away from her husband and children
- A teacher who sexually abused some students
- A couple who disagreed over money, social life, or how to manage children

I could go on and on. The range of human behavior because of sinful hearts seems endless. I suppose the most serious are couples and parents who neglect each other and their children.

God loves them all. None of these people deserve His love. They are all sinners—just a prayer away from a new start.

God's Spirit in Uganda

What Could I Say?

A bloody civil war raged in Uganda. There were shortages of food, water, vehicles, gasoline, and clothing. The roads had potholes the size of a car. Everywhere we looked there were ugly war machines: tanks, trucks, artillery. We had to pass through frequent checkpoints manned by armed teenaged soldiers. We were stopped twelve times while driving the twenty-five miles from the Entebbe airport to the capital city of Kampala. Each checkpoint made us open our bags for inspection.

The next day we were to travel to the city of Goma, where I was scheduled to address a meeting. Sam, my driver, had been scouring in vain to find some gasoline for our vehicle. We were three hours late when Sam finally came to me to say he found some gas for $30 per gallon. We needed fifteen gallons, or $450 worth.

I questioned our going. Who would wait for a foreign speaker who is three hours late? Sam convinced me we should go. It was a slow, bumpy ride, and there were more roadblocks manned by unfriendly soldiers. We arrived at a meeting place packed with people. It was so hot and humid that the air in the room was almost unbearable.

I sat on the platform, looking out at the audience. I knew most of them were hungry. They were shabbily dressed. I knew no one in this audience had stood in front of a closet packed full of clothes and wondered what to wear. What could I say to these people when I had never wondered what I would eat or wear? I knew that many of them had suffered the death of a family member. Many of their families were scattered, some having fled into the forest to avoid being mowed down by hostile gunfire. I prayed silently, "Lord, I don't know what to say to these people. God, You have to help me."

The only thought that came to me was:

> But the fruit of the Spirit is love, joy, peace, longsuffering, kindness, goodness, faithfulness, gentleness, self-control. Against such there is no law.
>
> Gal. 5:22–23

I told them I believed that each one of them could have all they wanted of a free gift. The gift was the fruit of the Spirit. It was freely available to all people.

An Important Message

After the meeting, a raggedly dressed man approached me. He said I seemed uncertain about my message. He reassured me that the fruit of the Spirit was available in Uganda, but I had left an important condition out of my message. He asked me if I would take the time to come to his home. He would like to tell me his story.

As we walked down a dusty road in the intense heat, he pointed to a large house, with perhaps five or six bedrooms, up in the hills. "That was my house," he said, "but Idi Amin's soldiers came one day and took it as headquarters for his army. My family had to flee, and today they are in the forest. I had a Mercedes-Benz parked in front of my clothing store. One day the soldiers came and took my car. Then they took my store."

We had been walking on this dusty road lined with mud-walled huts with thatched roofs. We came to one, and he indicated that this was where he lived. We entered it: one dark room, dirt floor, and a box on the floor. He motioned me to sit on the box. He sat on the other end of it and continued his story.

"I would sit in my chair and work myself into a frenzy over the soldiers who took my car, my business, my house, and scattered my family. I was consumed with hatred, bitterness, and anger.

"When I was forced to leave my house, I took along a chair. I had a cow, also, which needed some fly spray. I traded my chair for the fly spray, but my cow died. I also had a goat and traded my goat for some seeds to plant a garden. But it didn't rain, so my garden failed. Now I have no car, no business, no house, no family, no chair, no cow, no goat, no garden.

"One day, as I sat on this box and rehearsed all of this, I thought I would burst with hatred and animosity. A man came to my door in the middle of this situation. He said he was a missionary and had come to tell me that God loved me. That's all I heard. 'God loves me?' I exploded. 'Do you know what has happened to me?'

"In a rage, I picked that man up and threw him out of my house. God loves me! I was so mad I could hardly contain myself! To my surprise, the man got up and came back in. I was startled at his boldness. He said he had come to tell me about Jesus and would like to continue. He told me, 'God loves you so much that He gave His own Son to die for you. If you ask Him, He will come into your life and change your heart.'

"I was furious! Then suddenly, what this man said gave me some hope. I needed something, so I asked Jesus to come into my life right then. He did.

"Now I come to the part of my story that has to do with your message. I told you that something was missing.

"When I asked Jesus to come into my life, I could still see my home occupied by soldiers, my Mercedes-Benz being driven by soldiers, my business ruined, my family scattered, without a garden, and wondering how to survive. My heart was still filled with animosity toward those soldiers. My new friend read me a Bible verse intended for children of God:

> '"For if you forgive men their trespasses, your heavenly Father will also forgive you. But if you do not forgive men their trespasses, neither will your Father forgive your trespasses."'
>
> Matt. 6:14–15

"A shaft of light into utter darkness! I needed to forgive those soldiers. I needed to love them. Suddenly I wanted to love them. I opened my heart and poured out all the hate and anger and bitterness that I had stored up there. All I wanted was the fruit of the Spirit in my heart.

"You are right," he said. "We can have all we want for free. But you must meet God's terms. You must forgive men their trespasses."

My new friend said he was the richest man in Uganda. He had been released from the unbearable load of sin (hate, anger, bitterness) and now was basking in the unlimited wealth of the fruit of the Spirit that only God can give. As we parted, I promised him that I would share his story with others.

The Condition of My Heart

As I walked away, I remembered a man who had never paid me back some money I had lent him. I had nursed a grudge against him for a long time. (Webster's defines a grudge as a "cherished ill will with deep resentment at a real or imagined slight.") I, too, had to release that grudge; I did after a struggle similar to my new friend's struggle in Uganda. The man still owed me the money, but what a difference to love a debtor instead of hating him.

My new friend faced greater problems than most of us can imagine. How foolish it was to add the pain resulting from hate, anger, and bitterness when he could change them for peace, joy, love, kindness, and forgiveness.

I can be just as angry over my little problems as my friend could be over his big ones. The fact that a man did not pay me back my money did not determine what was in my heart. His decision only revealed the condition of my heart. The money issue is between the man and me. The condition of my heart is between God and me.

I will never forget the man from Uganda who took the time to minister to me. In order for any of us to experience the fruit of the Spirit, we must let go of our pet grudges. For him, it meant to forgive those unnamed soldiers. For me, it was someone who failed to repay a debt owed to me.

I needed to forgive, which forced me to examine my heart. If there was anger, hatred, the desire for revenge, or physical attack, then I had to deal with *myself* before I could deal with the offense. I was so preoccupied with the offense that I fail to recognize my own need. Jesus once advised a multitude:

> "Why do you look at the speck in your brother's eye, but do not consider the plank in your own eye? Hypocrite! First remove the plank from your own eye, and then you will see clearly to remove the speck from your brother's eye."
>
> Matt. 7:3, 5

To try to live the Christian life without total dependence on the Holy Spirit is a contradiction in terms. Anything less is just acting. Paul's words are true:

> And my God shall supply all your need according to His riches in glory by Christ Jesus.
>
> Phil. 4:19

> Be filled with the Spirit.
>
> Eph. 5:18

We want to be self-sufficient and independent. Many people have enough self-control to act the way they choose to act. They can rightly say, "Now that I know what to do, I will act like a Christian." They think they are in total control of their own lives. What they have is only a sad counterfeit that appears to be a cure.

Has a grudge ever helped you?

> Be gentle and ready to forgive; never hold grudges. Remember, the Lord forgave you, so you must forgive others.
>
> Col. 3:13, TLB

To forgive and to be forgiven go hand in hand. When someone trespasses against us, we usually must deal with our own sins as well as with the other person.

But people want to know when it is acceptable not to forgive. We are confronted on all sides with stories of physical and sexual abuse, rape, unfaithfulness, stealing, suffering, swindling. The list is long. Is no one entitled to withhold forgiveness? Why should we forgive such treatment? The answer is clear.

Forgiveness freed my friend from the nonproductive and destructive emotions which chained him and enslaved him to the object of his anger. He found that forgiveness was the foundation of good mental health.

> These things I have spoken to you, that in Me you may have peace. In the world you will have tribulation; but be of good cheer, I have overcome the world.
>
> John 16:33

A Word of Caution

Psychology books classify both anger and joy as emotions. Yet in the Bible, anger (literally, "fits of rage") is called an act of the sinful nature. Joy is called a fruit of the Spirit. It doesn't take a theologian to conclude that if you elevate one work of the flesh as "God-given," then you should do the same for all of them. Lust, deceit, drunkenness, witchcraft, and covetousness would all qualify. I rather believe these are a result of sin in the garden of Eden.

You cannot merely decide to become angry. Sooner or later your anger is triggered. When you are aware of anger in your body, you will be forced to do something to manage that anger.

The Christian has two options: (1) to repent—recognizing that anger is sin—and to yield self to the cleansing and empowering ministry of the Holy Spirit; or (2) to attempt to manage the anger in the sinful heart. It is self-control versus a lifetime dependence on Spirit-control. These are opposites.

187

Remember Mr. Hartley? A cursing employee triggered his anger (sin). A therapist could help him learn how to change from expressing his anger in destructive ways and learn to develop new behavior patterns that would enable him to express his anger in constructive, satisfying ways. Tragically, many Christians turn to therapy (humanism) for relief from a sinful heart instead of turning to God for a cure.

To repeat, God commands us to walk in His Spirit. We are ordered to love evil people. If we were supposed to be angry at every evil encountered, we would be angry most of the time.

A Plan for Repentance

Jesus died for the president of the United States, members of Congress, governors, mayors, judges, lawyers, stockbrokers, CEOs, drug dealers, alcohol and tobacco manufacturers, prostitutes, pornography dealers, men, women, and children.

Why? Because He loved them!

Repentance for anger as sin is rare. Jesus explained why:

> "This is the verdict: Light has come into the world, but men loved darkness instead of light because their deeds were evil. Everyone who does evil hates the light, and will not come to the light for fear that his deeds will be exposed."
>
> John 3:19–20, NIV

Unrepentant, intelligent people believe that they can justify their anger because God gets angry. This is why they comb the Gospels for any shred of evidence that Jesus got angry. The term "righteous indignation" just blurs the issue.

Perhaps 95 percent of anyone's anger is plain, old-fashioned sin, and we all know it. Anger plagues everyone. We should simply face it and take Jesus up on His offer: "Come to Me, all you who labor and are heavy laden, and I will give you rest" (Matt. 11:28).

◆

Notes

1. *The American Heritage Dictionary*, 1992, s.v. "anger."
2. Edward Adam Strecker, *Discovering Ourselves* (New York: Macmillan, 1958), 114–15.
3. W. Phillip Keller, *A Shepherd Looks at the Good Shepherd and His Sheep* (Grand Rapids, Mich.: Zondervan Pub. House, 1978), 128–29.

12

Deceit and Hypocrisy

Deceit is the deliberate attempt to mislead someone. Hypocrisy is the pretended possession of those qualities that would make others believe in one's sincerity, goodness, devotion, etc.

Stolen Raspberries

When I was a boy, we lived in the suburbs. A neighbor had a fine raspberry patch. My instructions were to stay out of it unless permission was given by my parents and the people who owned the patch.

One day when there was no one around, I slipped into the patch and started eating the ripe, juicy raspberries. What a pleasure!

Suddenly, there was a noise behind me. I turned around and was face-to-face with the owner. Instantly, I was a bundle of tensions. My heart pounded wildly, and I began to sweat.

Desperately, I pleaded with the lady not to tell my mother. But she wouldn't promise. Those berries suddenly felt like a rock in my stomach as I headed away from the scene of the crime. For the rest of the day, a nagging question plagued my mind: Had she told my mother? I had a miserable afternoon.

This was a conscious, deliberate choice to do wrong. Now, I was suffering agony because of it. Soon, I heard my mother call:

"Hennnnnnnnnrrrrrreeeee!"

"Yes, Mom." Scared to death. Here it comes.

"Henry, I want you to go to the store."

What a relief! Maybe she didn't know. But how could I tell? At dinner, I was fidgety and nervous. Finally, my father said:

"What's wrong with you?"

"Nothing wrong with me, Dad. Nothing at all. Nothing." I realized I had protested too much.

"Then, why don't you eat?"

"I'm eating."

I was eating but the food gave me a sick feeling. I glanced nervously back and forth between my father and mother. Finally, she said:

"Henry, there is too something wrong with you."

"Nothing wrong, Mom." I resisted the temptation to say it again, then got out of there as quickly as possible.

It was a terrible evening. The frightening climax came when Dad called. Usually, when he called me something was up. Again, there was the same reaction within me—tension, sweating, and a pounding heart.

"It's bedtime!" was all he said.

Whew! What a relief to disappear into the bedroom. But, it proved to be a most uncomfortable night.

The next day I was playing outside and, to my dismay, here came the lady who owned the raspberry patch. I ducked behind a corner of the house, and spied on her as she approached.

She came closer. Closer. Closer.

Then, she went past the house. And on down the street.

So it went for days of agonized misery. And I never did find out if she told my parents.

I've listened to countless stories in the consulting room of people who create similar tensions for themselves because of their own actions. No one knows their secret. But they know. And that's enough.

Smoking Pocket

Your secret may not be that you robbed a bank or murdered someone. It can be as simple as sneaking into a raspberry patch.

When we do so, we must live with whatever tension goes with it—sometimes much and sometimes little. You don't break God's laws (disobey authority) without paying a personal price of inner tension.

Some years ago, I taught a college-age Sunday School class. One young man in the class often said:

"I am very devoted to the Lord. Because my body is the Lord's, I want to take care of it. I don't stay up late, I'm careful what I eat, I exercise regularly, don't drink, smoke, or chase women."

We all listened and nodded. It's good to know that your students take your teaching seriously.

"Good for you," we would say.

Then, one day at an airport many miles from home, I thought I saw this model student standing in front of the building.

Guess what?

He had a cigar in his mouth, puffing away as happy as could be. He didn't notice me. Since he was in my Sunday School class, I walked up to chat with him. Then he saw me—and did a very strange thing.

He stuck that cigar—still smoking—in his pocket!

Isn't a pocket a strange place to put a lighted cigar? He was not very happy to see me. One would think he would be glad to see his Sunday School teacher, especially this far from home.

Exactly the opposite. He was in a hurry to be off.

As we talked, the smoke began curling up from his pocket.

What was wrong? He was the architect of his own misery. His conduct did not fit his words.

A Scripture verse pointedly summarizes the personal benefit of practicing righteousness: "You love righteousness and hate wickedness; therefore God, your God, has by anointing you with the oil of joy" set you above your companions (Ps. 45:7, NIV).

The First Act of Concealment

Phillips Brooks gave a positive basis for happy living:

> To keep clear of concealment, to keep clear of the need of concealment, to do nothing which he might not do out on the middle of Boston Common at noonday—I cannot say how more and more that seems to me to be the glory of a young man's life.

It is an awful hour when the first necessity of hiding something comes. The whole life is different thenceforth.

When there are questions to be feared and eyes to be avoided and subjects which must not be touched, then the bloom of life is gone. Put off that day as long as possible. Put it off forever if you can. Can your actions stand publicity?

Everyone interacts with other people—in a family, at work, at church, in a store, in a car, in a neighborhood. In the process, you either reveal or conceal what is on your mind.

Deception Is Common

An anxious, disgruntled young man—married six months—came to see me about his marriage. He hated his wife's hair-do, her cooking, housekeeping, and lovemaking. What was he doing about it?

"I haven't the heart to tell her, Dr. Brandt. So I have been telling her what a good job she has been doing in each of those areas."

A very worried and tense young lady came to see me because her wedding date was two months away, and she could not stand her boyfriend. He was tied to his family, wasted his money, and did not bathe often enough.

What was she doing about the problem? Nothing. Instead, she told him how much she loved and admired him and gave everyone the impression that she was thrilled about the upcoming marriage.

Many of my counselees appear to be radiantly happy when they enter the consulting room, but before the session is over they reveal a bitter, hateful spirit.

I have often been in social gatherings also attended by my counselees. Some of the most bitter ones appear to be the happiest people there.

All these people were prepared to do anything to avoid the hatred, anger, ill will, or the critical spirit of another person to be directed at them—even to the point of lying and deceiving.

Why? Because their sense of self-respect depended on the goodwill of the other person. But a deceitful relationship is self-defeating. These people did not come to see me because the other person was dissatisfied. They came because they, themselves, were miserable.

Perjury

In the courtroom, if a witness fails to reveal accurately what is on his mind, it is called perjury. The Watergate scandal should be a stark reminder of the misery we can cause ourselves by covering up the truth. The men involved brought the wrath of the nation down on themselves.

In day-to-day, human relations, we tend to create minor Watergates when we misrepresent what is on our minds and hearts. We can give ourselves a variety of reasons for practicing such deception. Some are:

- My friend would hate me.
- My mother would be upset.
- My father would be angry.
- My teacher would flunk me.
- My boss would fire me.
- My friends would be hurt or surprised.
- My church would ask me to leave.

When you misrepresent yourself to others—that is, when you lie and deceive others, for any reason—you violate a commandment:

Putting away lying, "Let each one of you speak truth with his neighbor," for we are members of one another.

Eph. 4:25

To deceive another is to chip away at your own self-respect, even though you receive praise and good will as a result.

If someone is nursing hatred or wrath in his heart and then discovers that he has been deceived, he will shower that wrath on whoever deceived him just as surely as the nation showered its wrath on the Watergate people.

You err when your sense of self-respect is based on the spiritual condition of another person. You build your own self-respect when your words, behavior, emotions, and mental activity line up with God's commandments.

> The heart knows its own bitterness, and a stranger does not share its joy.
>
> Prov. 14:10

Only you know what goes on underneath your skin. Whether bitterness or joy floods your soul is known only to you. I have spent a lifetime studying people, and am fully convinced that I cannot accurately decide what goes on in someone else's heart and mind.

First Impressions

A janitor walked in on a nursery school at his church. The children were working on cutouts; paper scraps littered the floor. Gruffly, he ordered:

"You kids clean up this paper, or I'll throw you into the furnace!"

The teacher, who was new to the school, gasped. But the children ran gleefully into his outstretched arms. They knew that all he meant was, "Hello, kids, I'm glad to see you!"

From what the janitor said, the teacher got a totally wrong impression of his attitude toward children.

I am impressed by the wisdom given to us by the apostle Paul:

But why do you judge your brother? Or why do you show contempt for your brother? For we shall all stand before the judgment seat of Christ. For it is written, "As I live, says the LORD, every knee shall bow to Me, and every tongue shall confesst to God." So then each of us shall give account of himself to God. Therefore let us not judge one another anymore, but rather resolve this, not to put a stumbling block or a cause to fall in our brother's way.

Rom. 14:10–13

You can hear what I say and observe what I do, but you cannot judge the *accuracy* of what I say, nor can you judge my motives or my sincerity. You and I must stand or fall before God alone, when it comes to our mental activity. How, then, can we know each other? Only as we choose to open our minds and hearts to one another.

I appeal to you, brothers, in the name of our Lord Jesus Christ, that all of you agree with one another so that there may be no divisions among you and that you may be perfectly united in mind and in thought.

1 Cor. 1:10, NIV

Therefore if there is any consolation in Christ, if any comfort of love, if any fellowship of the Spirit, if any affection and mercy, fulfill my joy by being likeminded, having the same love, being of one accord, of one mind.

Phil. 2:1–2

Contained in the verses mentioned above is a description of the mental activity involved in maintaining fellowship.

He Thinks—He Says

"Like-minded" is stated as "agreement, no divisions, same mind, same judgment, same love, and one purpose." If your minds are not together, you are not together, even if you speak the same words and do the same things. To better understand, look at these illustrations:

He Thinks:

Her hair is pretty

He Says:

"I like your hairdo."

Delicious food

"Your cooking is great!"

His mind agrees with his words. He is communicating accurately. Here is another illustration:

He thinks:	He says:	She says:	She thinks:
Hungry	"I'm hungry!"	"So am I."	*Hungry*
McDonalds	"Where do you want to go?"	"Anywhere"	*Steak House*
McDonalds	"Let's go to McDonalds."	"I don't want to. Let's go to the Steak House."	*Steak House*

He thinks:	He says:	She says:	She thinks:

| *I hate this.* | "OK" | "I'm pleased." | *He's agreed.* |

He and she were both hungry and agreed to go out. She said she would go anywhere, but she did not mean it and admitted it.

He agreed verbally to go to the steak house, but he did not change his mind. To that extent, he deceived her, and they were not like-minded. What should he have done? He could have said, "I'd rather not go the steak house but I will."

Why is that so important? He is telling the truth, rather than deceiving her.

Audrey and Ralph

Audrey was known as a good neighbor, a cheerful wife, and a generous, considerate person who loved to go out of her way to be helpful.

Ralph was proud of his cheerful, neighborly wife, who never fussed at him, even when he brought guests home on short notice. In the consulting room, she said, "I'm a very unhappy person." I came to find out why.

Is it not strange that Audrey was more concerned about appearing to be cheerful and generous than really being cheerful and generous? This intelligent woman did not seem to realize the difference between acting and being real. Her invisible, but very heavy, burden was self-centeredness and

She Thinks:	She Says:
 *Oh, no. Not again!*	"I'd be glad to entertain your guests."
I hate this.	"So good to have you over after church."

deception. She called it neighborliness and cooperation. How true these verses are:

> "The heart is more deceitful than all else and is desperately sick; who can understand it? I, the Lord, search the heart, I test the mind, even to give to each man according to his ways."

Jer. 17:9–10, NASB

Like so many of us, all Audrey needed was some instruction. No one needed to tell her that all her hard work only produced more personal misery. She saw where she was wrong and asked God to replace her selfish, deceitful spirit with His spirit of truth and service. Put in a Bible verse:

> The purpose of the commandment is love from a pure heart, from a good conscience, and from sincere faith.

1 Tim. 1:5

Then she worked out a more realistic schedule with her husband and neighbors. This was not as easy as it sounds. First, she had to admit to Ralph that much of her friendly cooperation was just plain phoniness. He did not take it very well at first, but it was true, and he had to live with it.

Second, Audrey and Ralph needed to negotiate a new plan. This was not easy either. Ralph was so accustomed to Audrey's agreeing with everything, he had to get used to contrary opinions coming from her. Ralph, in the past, could easily get his own opinion accepted, it seemed, but now he frequently heard her say:

"You have not changed my mind. "That was a stopper when they came to a deadlock.

Third, they had to learn to settle deadlocks—that is, making decisions knowing that their opinions differed. In such cases, one of them had to make the decision, and the other had to concede.

In the long run, Audrey and Ralph built a good marriage on the firm foundation of truth.

> Being of the same mind, maintaining the same love, united in spirit, intent on one purpose.
>
> Phil. 2:2, NASB

Separate Opinions

If your minds are divided, you are not together. I recall meeting a man at a conference who was talked into attending against his will. He was there in body but not in mind and left in two days.

A lady told me how she despised the dress she was wearing. She hated the color, but her husband made her wear it.

These people illustrate the struggle that goes on in our minds. If fellowship is the goal, this mental conflict must cease. There are a variety of ways to come to a meeting of minds:

1. agreement
2. concession
3. compromise
4. acceptance of authority

Two or more people decide, without mental reservations, to drive to New York next Tuesday and stay at a Hampton Inn for a week. This could be called an *agreement*.

If someone in the party prefers a Sheraton Inn, but finally agrees to the Hampton Inn, this is a *concession*, provided the decision is made without mental reservations.

On the way to New York, the travelers take turns driving. One drives 50 mph, the other 70 mph. One's speed is too slow to suit the other, and the other's speed is too fast for his partner. So, they agree to both drive 60 mph. This is a *compromise*.

The travelers differ over how often to stop along the way and where to eat. Finally, they agree that there must be a leader who has the last word, and one of them is chosen to be the leader. The leader decides to give the traveling partner the responsibility for deciding where to eat. The leader will decide when to stop. This is *accepting authority*.

No person can separate feelings, thoughts, and actions as we have done in this book. This is especially true when differences of opinion arise. We all tend to go our own way, and our opinions will sooner or later collide with someone else's. So to work on being like-minded is a continuous process, and the process will reveal the spirit.

Constant changes force us to make adjustments. All require daily decisions. The necessity for making these decisions calls for a certain attitude as described by this verse:

Let nothing be done through selfish ambition or empty conceit, but in lowliness of mind let each esteem others as more important than himself.

Phil. 2:3

Negotiating new agreements can be fun only if you approach one another unselfishly, humbly, and keep the importance of the other person in mind.

When there is a difference of opinion and you are not walking in the Spirit, it is easy to lose sight of the importance of the other person and become preoccupied with the negative side of the person you are negotiating with.

In marriage counseling, I have observed that a couple contemplating marriage cannot say enough good about the partner, who has become the most important person in the world.

But in the consulting room, because they are no longer like-minded, all they can think of is what is wrong with the partner. This negative way of thinking can happen whenever there is a clash of opinion, even though the qualities of the opponent are still there.

In the effort to come to a meeting of minds, you tend to get caught up in your own interest and lose sight of the other person's. Remember, to come to a meeting of minds implies a difference of opinion in the first place.

> Do not merely look out for your own personal interests, but also for the interests of others.
>
> Phil. 2:4, NASB

The Servant Attitude

We once moved to a home with a large picture window overlooking some water. Eva wanted drapes on the window, and I did not. We discussed the issue back and forth. She even proved to me that everyone we know had drapes on their windows. After everything that could be said on both sides was said, she still wanted drapes, and I did not. A decision had to be made. Being the head of the family, it was my decision. The result?

We installed the drapes.

Why?

Eva spent more time in that home than I did. I wanted to please her, and she wanted drapes. Since it is only a matter of opinion, and considering her interests as well as mine, the drapes did not affect the view. It just made sense to yield to her interest. That settled it. We came to a meeting of minds.

> Have this attitude in yourselves which was also in Christ Jesus, who, although He existed in the form of God, did not regard equality with God a thing to be grasped, but emptied Himself, taking the form of a bond-servant, and being made in the likeness of men. And being found in appearance as a man, He humbled Himself by becoming obedient to the point of death, even death on a cross.
>
> Phil. 2:5–8, NASB

Such is the attitude of a servant toward whomever is served. Jesus was special—the Son of God, the creator of the universe. Yet He gave Himself fully to His task. He did not need to. He just surrendered Himself.

You are also special, with talent, ability, creativity, training. You have power, influence, perhaps riches. You may be smarter than the person you are negotiating with.

I used to think that servants are people who have lowly positions with low pay. When I was a boy, my mother would take in washings and scrub floors. I would deliver the washings to these huge homes. There were maids, cooks, chauffeurs, gardeners. In my youthful mind, these people were servants.

Now, I see it differently. Physicians, teachers, counselors, lawyers, builders, and bankers are servants, too. They make lots of money. It is not the pay that makes you a servant. It is the giving of yourself totally to your task.

This spirit is required if you are to be like-minded. You give yourself totally and completely to find a basis for a meeting of minds with whomever you must cooperate.

Training, ability, power, or wealth do not exempt you from making a continuous effort to maintain like-mindedness—even unto death.

Managing Your Inner Life

The management of your inner life is, to me, the most important subject in this book. Every day you will either reveal or conceal feelings, emotions, attitudes, intentions, and thoughts stimulated by people and events. Either way, whether you reveal or conceal, there they are, coming from within you.

You cannot control what other people do around you. Neither can you control all the events of the day. How you respond will either build up or chip away at your self-respect and self-love, depending on how you manage what goes on underneath your skin.

A woman approached me about her husband. They had been married twenty years. They were active in religious circles; he was even an elder in the church. But he kept a bottle of vodka in his office and was usually tipsy when he came home. He demanded a hot meal every night, even though his arrival time was unpredictable. Then he expected her to sit with him to watch television and pour his drinks for him.

Since the children were out of the house, this relationship had become unbearable. She had never complained to her husband, she said, and faithfully served him. But she was consumed with rebellion, resentment, and anger. She could not stand it much longer!

I pointed out to her that she had two problems. Her husband was obviously one of them. He was inconsiderate, selfish, and demanding. But her most serious problem was what went on inside her.

"But I have served him faithfully," she protested. It did appear that her behavior was beyond criticism. She doggedly was living up to the letter of the law. But, God's Spirit was missing.

"But my husband just thinks about himself."

I listen to this line of reasoning constantly. "My inner life is caused by people or circumstances. How else do you expect me to respond? Am I supposed to enjoy such treatment? Haven't I put up with this long enough? Don't I deserve some consideration, too?"

This woman was convinced that her inner life was in the hands of her husband. Several months later, I received a letter from her. It is printed here (in part):

> Nothing has changed in our marriage, but I am contented. I felt so angry with you for what you said to me about myself—but you were right!
>
> Before that, I hadn't really recognized my own sin. God had to do some throwing down in my life, and that is never easy at the time. But the result is beautiful if you are submissive to the strong hand of God.
>
> He has forgiven and cleansed and filled my heart with joy. I praise Him for this mercy and grace. Once again, I want to say "thank you" from the depths of my heart.

Her letter illustrates the Scripture:

> "And this is the condemnation, that the light has come into the world, and men loved the darkness rather than light, because their deeds were evil. For everyone practicing evil hates the light and does not come to the light, lest his deeds should be exposed. But he who does the truth comes to the light, that his deeds may be clearly seen, that they have been done in God."
>
> John 3:19–21

There it is. We are at least vaguely aware of our evil inner life, but we hate to admit it. We tend to turn away from such light. The more brilliant and educated we are, the more we are capable of coming up with endless varieties of ways to justify ourselves.

Enough of this gloom. There is a brighter side. There is hope. When we finally quit running, the Lord will search our hearts, show us our evil ways, clean us up, and fill us with His strength.

Like any other agreement, this step is taken at a point in time never to be forgotten or confused with other times. But such a crisis works itself out from a point to a line. It involves a continual drawing upon His resources as each occasion for it comes, just as a decision to maintain an exercise program must be renewed day by day.

Becoming a Truthful Person

In conclusion, take a look at the riches available to you in the inner man—which will build your self-respect, your self-love.

Be kind to one another, tenderhearted, forgiving one other, even as as God in Christ forgave you.

Eph. 4:32

Therefore, as the elect of God, holy and beloved, put on tender mercies, kindness, humility, meekness, longsuffering and patience; bearing with one another, and forgiving one another, if anyone has a complaint against another; even as Christ forgave you, so you also must do.

Col. 3:12–13

Love is patient, love is kind, and is not jealous; love does not brag and is not arrogant, does not act unbecomingly;

it does not seek its own, is not provoked, does not take into account a wrong suffered, does not rejoice in unrighteousness, but rejoices with the truth; bears all things, believes all things, hopes all things, endures all things. Love never fails.

1 Cor. 13:4–8, NASB

Here are some of the qualities contained in these verses, laid out on an imaginary cafeteria counter: kind, tenderhearted, forgiveness, compassionate, humble, gentle, patient, peaceful, thankful, reasonable, merciful, unhypocritical, not jealous, or envious.

Help yourself. It is all free. The more you take, the farther along you will be on your way to becoming a truthful person.

◆

13

Humanism

Frequently a minister will approach me to inquire what he should read in order to better understand the nature of humanism. So far, he has only studied theology. He is curious about the social sciences.

The answer is pro and con. Yes, there is material available that can be very helpful: methodology in conducting an interview, recording the content of interviews, helps to improve public speaking or teaching, time and money management, rules for managing a staff, and training techniques.

By definition, the social sciences study how people affect one another as they interact with one another. Belief in God's intervening in human affairs is not a consideration. Accordingly, the Bible is also not considered. Note that the biblical view of man is not discussed. It is not ruled out; *it is not considered.*

A student of the social sciences will note that the description of how people behave and interact with each other is the same as described in the Bible. What is easily overlooked is that the cause and cure differ.

Since the description of human behavior is the same, the Bible student must be careful not to get swept along and accept the cause and cure proposed in the social sciences. A few comparisons will be useful to understand where we differ.

The Human Ideal

The Bible and secular psychology are in general agreement. Qualities such as love, joy, peace, long-suffering, kindness, goodness, faithfulness, gentleness, and self-control are basic and necessary if human beings are to live together harmoniously.

The humanist believes that the human being possesses the power and the ability to experience these qualities. The process for developing these qualities is through reliance on intelligence, the scientific method, social cooperation, and faith in the essential decency of mankind.

The Christian believes that the human being does not possess the power and ability to experience these qualities. They are readily available to human beings and are the work of the Holy Spirit of God. *The source of these qualities is out of this world.* The process involves a transaction between God and a human being. No one can force a person or stop a person from seeking these qualities from God.

This view is nonsense to the humanist. This is a good time to review a biblical basis for our faith. Review chapter 3.

> And be found in Him, not having my own righteousness, which comes from the law, but that which is through faith in Christ, the righteousness which is from God by faith.
>
> Phil. 3:9

For the kingdom of God is not eating and drinking, but righteousness and peace and joy in the Holy Spirit. For he who serves Christ in these things is acceptable to God and approved by men.

Rom. 14:17–18

May the God of hope fill you with all joy and peace as you trust in him, so that you may overflow with hope by the power of the Holy Spirit.

Rom. 15:13, NIV

But the fruit of the Spirit is love, joy, peace, longsuffering, kindness, goodness, faithfulness, gentleness, self-control. Against such there is no law.

Gal. 5:22–23

Strengthened with all might according to His glorious power, for all patience and joy.

Col. 1:11

But the wisdom that comes from heaven is first of all pure; then peace-loving, considerate, submissive, full of mercy and good fruit, impartial and sincere.

James 3:17, NIV

Grace and peace be multiplied to you in the knowledge of God and of Jesus our Lord, as His divine power has given to us all things that pertain to life and godliness, through the knowledge of Him who called us by glory and virtue.

2 Pet. 1:2–3

Human Maladjustment

There is general agreement between humanists and Christians that behavior patterns such as evil thoughts, pride, hate, anger, deceit, dissension, slander (malicious misrepresentation), theft, selfishness, drunkenness, and sexual immorality are self-defeating and unhealthy.

Humanists believe such behavior has its origin outside the person, as a product of human experience within a culture. The human being has within himself the power and ability to correct these responses through reliance on intelligence, the scientific method, social cooperation and faith in the essential decency of mankind.

The Christian believes that human experience within a culture stirs up such behavior which has its roots within the human being, called the acts of the sinful nature, or sin. The Christian says there is no human remedy for sin within the person. *The solution involves God and the person.*

The Christian view is nonsense to the humanist. To declare that human beings need a supernatural change of heart and a lifetime dependence on the power of God is an insult to humanistic thinking.

To the Christian, self-cleansing and/or obeying God's commandment through reliance on essential human decency, intelligence, or social cooperation is an impossibility.

Basis for Humanistic Optimism

A brief look at our world makes it obvious that the human being has some basis for declaring ourselves self-sufficient, for declaring that there is no God and that we must save ourselves.

In my lifetime I have seen the astonishing development of the radio, television, computers, telephone, the automobile, airplanes, and construction industries. There has been spectacular progress in medicine. I could go on and on to describe the remarkable discoveries made by people.

If intelligence, scientific method, and human cooperation produced this wonderful world, the same method should be capable of solving human relations problems. It seems reasonable, doesn't it? We should be able to help ourselves.

My first encounter with people who declared there is no God was when I entered graduate school. My professors were highly trained, thoughtful, dedicated people. In my clinical psychology classes we grappled with the challenge of helping disturbed people—people who were hostile, hateful, resentful, rebellious, frustrated, confused, angry, cruel, selfish, dishonest, and destructive.

We were taught that a person is a biological organism whose total personality is a product of functioning in a social and cultural environment. What in the world can be changed or given to release this person from a prison of destructive emotions and behavior?

The humanist and the biblically oriented person agree generally on the definition of the problem.

At this point we came to a fork in the road. Our guidebook is the Bible. The very words that the humanist uses to describe destructive emotions and behavior are put under one heading in the Bible—*sin*. Society only brings out of us what is already there. We affirm that there is no human remedy for sin. You need a Savior who will cleanse you from sin and empower you to walk in the Spirit (love, joy, peace, long-suffering, goodness, faithfulness, kindness, gentleness, self-control). Sin is the simplest problem there is to deal with because Jesus died for our sins. (Chapter 3 goes into more detail.) When Jesus announced that He came to save His people from their sins, people crucified Him.

Today, if we declare that the reason for disturbed behavior is sinfulness, we will hear a cry of resistance from intelligent, educated, influential, politically powerful people who have the best interests of humanity at heart—people who firmly and fiercely reject the concept of sin, a Savior, and a God.

Government agencies, mental health agencies, educators, law enforcement agencies, parents, individuals face this problem every day. What can be done to help restless, disturbed people become people whose response to life is more like the description of the fruit of the Spirit?

If it is indeed sin that we are dealing with, the question would be how to manage a sinful nature! The humanist is making some progress.

There is a supernatural way to change the sinful heart. The world says, for example, that alcoholism is a disease; you can manage this disease, but you cannot get rid of it. The world sees this as a kindly approach. At the same time, the world would say that Christians are harsh and unkind by saying that drunkenness is sin. Deceptive philosophy tries to show the Christian as harsh and the world as kind. However, the opposite is true. The Christians offer a real Cure—Christ! The world only offers management of ongoing problems.

◆

14

Truth, Professionalism, Servanthood

Some Christian psychology scholars say that all truth is God's truth—wherever it is found. Human literature and the Bible describe similar behavior patterns that, on the one hand, lead to peaceful, harmonious living, and on the other hand, are self-defeating and unhealthy. For example, the humanist would describe anger, hate, love, and joy as manageable human emotions. The Bible calls anger and hate acts of the sinful nature and love and joy the fruit of the Spirit. In dealing with these you will look at *the environment* if you follow the humanist. You will look *to God* if you follow the Bible.

Let me suggest an approach to evaluating truth. While awaiting His crucifixion, Jesus was praying for his disciples. He prayed:

"Sanctify them by Your truth. Your word is truth."

John 17:17

The Bereans were described as having noble character for this reason:

They received the message with great eagerness and examined the Scriptures every day to see if what Paul said was true.

Acts 17:11, NIV

These verses say that the Bible is the standard to evaluate the truth of any other literature or speech.

Some of my professors were as dedicated to serving people as anyone could be. But they were ungodly. They were good people, but they were humanists. They believed there is no God.

It follows that a student of the Bible will quickly sense that humanistic writing leads in a different direction than the Bible does. Without a Bible background, you have no basis for comparison.

Truth

Speaking the truth means to test what you are thinking by the Bible before you speak. Speaking truth in love is necessary. The truth itself is not enough. Sometimes I have counselees who are waiting for the truth so they can hit someone over the head with it. It is a wrong motivation for wanting truth.

I am amazed at myself and at other people who get nervous about dealing with the truth. In this world, we have learned to say the handy thing, the convenient thing, the diplomatic thing. Whether it is true or not is not so important. A person may ask me if I am knowledgeable about a subject. I may say, "Yes, I know something about that. But at this time I do not want to tell you about it." It is best not to pretend to not know something that I know.

I am dealing with a husband and a wife right now. She has three boyfriends. In my judgment, I do not think the husband can handle knowing that. I have warned him that communication between him and his wife is not what it ought to be. He does not know everything about his wife, but he should start finding out. All I will tell him is that he does not know all he needs to know. I will try to help him develop a basis whereby he can know, but I am not going to tell him. I must not lie or be deceitful. If I do, it is time for me confess my sin and ask God to straighten me out.

Discussion is not so valuable as people think, in my opinion. People can discuss anything. People have no idea of what they will be like when a child comes along—adjustments are made as they go. It is important for them to know themselves. People devise all kinds of lovely plans that never happen. Adjustment, change, inconsistency, is the stuff of life. People cannot expect their life to tick along smoothly.

Professionalism

If you love the people who come to you and are interested in helping them, that is a professional attitude.

Professionalism requires sticking to the point. To get straight to the point and not forget why they are there, yes. To have somebody come in and talk about a committee they are working on for fifteen minutes, no.

I counsel with people who are friends of mine. I distinguish between being their counselor and being their friend. We do not talk about other things when we are counseling. In that sense, we are being professional.

The Professional's Time

In counseling with ministers, I find that they tend to wander all over the place. It is hard to stick to the point. If you are going to do right by all of your people, you cannot waste a lot of time. You have too many people to deal with. I say to couples, "You have ten minutes left, then we must quit. My next hour is taken. I cannot see you for another week."

I do not know how many of you are married. I take my family responsibility very seriously, and I schedule time at home into my calendar. Someone will call up and ask to see me the very next day. I tell them, "My calendar is full tomorrow. I will be home with my family. I will see you Thursday." But they want to see me Wednesday! I find that it is very rare that somebody cannot wait another day. I think it is an insult to my wife to brush her aside. I am busy with other things. I find that my children need me. I have a life to live and I must keep a balance between my personal life and my work.

The time that you spend with your family depends on your family. Are they happy, wholesome, and easygoing? When you come home and see your children are getting in each other's hair, your wife is too tired, you had better tend to your home. If everything is fine and the kids are getting along well, maybe you do not need that much time. It is a question of judgment.

I must take time to be alone. I am not only a husband and a father, but I am also a person. My wife and my family may die in an automobile accident this week, yet I am still a person. My life must go on. In fact, coming to Chicago one day, I decided to take a train instead of a plane. That plane crashed. One decision was the difference between being here and being in heaven. But my wife's life would have gone on. She is a person as well as a wife. I should think that to be a helpful pastor requires you to be a wholesome person.

There were times when people could not see Jesus. He went alone to pray. Like Jesus, you must keep your life in balance. You must be realistic. I am not talking about loafing or pursuing your own selfish life. I am talking about replenishing your resources. There are times when you must readjust your schedule.

Yes, there are emergencies. Our children not only are our children, they are persons too. We expect our children to respect us as parents and as individuals. Our family does not revolve around our children. Our children are *part* of the family, and they have to adjust to adults as well as adults adjusting to them. Our children do not rule the roost at our house. But they have their rightful place.

Two plus two makes four, but so does three plus one. A little infant does not have the place that a teenager does. A teenager does not have the place that an adult does. Sometimes your child needs more of you than at other times. When the child needs you, you had better be there. If you do not have children, you have other demands. You are an example before other people.

I do believe that God comes first in my life. But the Bible says,

> Husbands, love your wives, just as Christ also loved the church.
>
> Eph. 5:25

What did He do for the church? He gave His very life for the church. It is up to me to give my very life to my family. That does not eliminate these other things. So far as my own relationship with my family, it is not so much quantity as it is quality of relationship. An hour of good wholesome relationship is a lot better than a day of strife.

There is no excuse for getting it out of balance. Oh, but there are so many people who want to see you. There are long-distance telephone calls coming in. Very good for your pride, but I think the Bible is clear about responsibilities of husbands to their wives and children. You must strike a balance.

You have other things to do besides counseling. In a business, the question is not, "Do I make the production department as efficient as possible and neglect the shipping department?" Stuff would be stacked all over the place. You must strike a balance.

You must limit the time you have for counseling. I could be at home counseling, but I may be writing or speaking. These, too, are my responsibilities. I cannot overdo either. I must limit the counseling that I can do. That means that some people must wait until next week or the week after, but we must keep a balance.

The Professional's Records

If you have records to keep, you should keep them as efficiently as you can. If you are too busy to keep records, you are too busy. If you can only counsel one afternoon a week, then counsel one afternoon a week. If you are so busy that you cannot give a student an hour, then give them half an hour. If you are sincerely busy and not just loafing, you will find that people will respect you and will wait to see you. You will get the reputation after a while that you will do all you can to help. You cannot be counseling with somebody and have your mind on records. You must give yourself to this situation:

> Whatever you do, do it heartily, as to the Lord and not to men.
>
> Col. 3:23

Servanthood

People struggle with the definition of a servant. If I hired a person to cook my meals and that person kept my flower beds neat and the lawn mowed and did the washing but did not cook my meals, I would say that servant is not doing the job. I did not hire a gardener. I hired a cook. In order to do the cooking, that cook has to say no to other things. Being a servant does not mean to just be a miscellaneous errand boy. If you are a good servant, you must do your job.

The Servant's Priorities

I think a preacher who is a good servant has to say sometimes, "I am sorry but I must stay home this morning to prepare my sermon for Sunday." I am not so sure that a preacher is being a good servant by running my errands for me because I will be mad at him if he does not do it. There is discipline to being a servant and a price to pay. That means that there are some things that you cannot do.

Right now I am doing an article. It is not finished, and I feel like a kid who did not turn in his English paper. I was hoping that I would not run into the editor. Yesterday I was standing in an elevator and the door opened and there he was. You must discipline yourself to accomplish anything constructive. Your mind and time easily can be taken up with extraneous details.

Every once in a while I get a letter in the mail asking me to go somewhere to resolve some problem. I did not ask for the letter, but it forces me to make a decision. A sense of being frantic and a sense of pressure would warn that I am out of touch with the peace of God. As I review the day, I must be able to say, "Well done", but almost invariably I have had to disappoint somebody. You cannot get away from it.

> If any of you lacks wisdom, he should ask God, who gives generously to all without finding fault, and it will be given to him.

James 1:5

You will not get away from making decisions but you have the privilege of speaking under God's guidance. Ultimately, your choices rest in your own lap. Certainly your relationship with God does.

Moses asked one time, "LORD, what will I do? Which way will I go? Give me some assurance that I am doing the right thing." God said to Moses, "My presence is with you." That is all the evidence he received. I believe that too, but God's presence is invisible. There is a sense of serenity, peace, joy and contentment if we walk in step with God. That involves making decisions. If you have any position at all, there is more to do in a day than you can do.

The Servant's Rest

You might say to yourself, "I am tired and I will take a rest tonight," but you feel guilty resting. You feel guilty whether you are entertaining or whether you are not. You feel guilty whether you are resting or working. You see, the problem is in yourself—you have not resolved this matter of serving the Lord. There is no rest. Do you get my point? There is something wrong with you, not your position, if you cannot come to a decision and be at rest about that decision. You may satisfy some people and not satisfy others and be at peace at the same time. What will give you authority as a counselor is the confidence in your own judgment and trusting that by faith this judgment of yours is ordained by God.

You may have submitted to God's will today. That does not imply that you will tomorrow. You may rebel tomorrow.

It is difficult. It is a dying-daily proposition to walk with God, and you struggle with it. I struggle with it, and you will continuously struggle with it. Remember that we are sinners who tend to go our own way. We are always voting. Who am I serving and who am I pleasing? God will reveal to us those things that are not right.

There are times when you must admit you were wrong. This business of working and relating yourself to people involves a continuous encounter with God. People walk into my office who are fuming when they walk in. It requires an ongoing submission to the power of God to face people like that.

I think we overrate our own importance. Psychiatrists say to be careful what you say. One wrong sentence can mislead a person for life. I do not have quite that much pride in myself that what I say is that important to anybody and will influence them for the rest of their life. However, someone may grab on to a sentence that I say and use it. I am often amazed at what people hear and what they do not hear in thirty minutes. But I do not get anxious about whether I will say the wrong thing or not. As best I know, I walk with God, I look to Him for wisdom, I am not too concerned about people's reactions. What I am concerned about is my reaction.

The Servant's Limitations

I cannot discern the response to my efforts. I often think an interview was a failure or a success. Then someone comes back, saying, "I was so mad at you yesterday I could have wrung your neck." I thought I was doing well. The important thing is that you are in the right spirit and that you are truthful.

People will say to you at two minutes to the half hour, "I just thought of something I must tell you." I get out my little book and say, "Let me see. You had better tell me on the 26th. Maybe you should write it down so that you do not forget it. We will continue then." All of us have our preconceived ideas about this. I think that there is definitely a point of diminishing returns in prolonging an interview.

I often have this kind of a discussion with a minister. He spent four hours counseling. I respond, "Four hours! What did you do that for?" He thought I would pat him on the back. Is that not terrific, spending four hours with somebody? I would never do it. I believe he lost his effectivenes long before the four hours was up. You cannot expose somebody to their troubles too long. When an hour is over, I say, "We have talked about this long enough. Here is the point we have made: Go home and process this with God and come back to discuss it next time."

I want to leave you with renewed respect for yourself, with some concept of the importance of your time and your own spirit's being the key to the whole thing. The amount of time you spend with people is not what is important. Too often your objective is to calm people down. Then we have been successful if they limp in and leap out. I do not care how they go out. I do not say that indifferently.

If within the limits of my time I cannot establish anything, I can only say, "I have nothing to go on after talking to you for an hour. You will have to come back." Some insist on talking about a certain thing when I think we have talked about it long enough. I say, "We will not talk about that anymore. I am the counselor. I must trust Gods wisdom as He directs me." Then I do a little guiding and switch topics. Counseling literature condemns this, but I urge you to give it a try. All I do is evaluate what I say in terms of the result. The rich young man came to Jesus and asked what he must do to be saved. Jesus told him to sell all he had. The Lord let him go away sorrowfully. It did not take long. There was something obviously wrong in the rich man's heart. Why look for something else?

A young man came to see me who was mad at his girl-friend. She had jilted him. I wanted to deal with the anger. I told him I could put him in touch with a power that would enable him to be free of this anger toward that girl. Would he be interested? Should I look for something else to talk about when there is something here as obvious as the nose on your face?

Counseling literature says that personality is subtle; unconscious motivations drive us; we do not really know what drives us. That may be true, but let us first eliminate the obvious problem. I am convinced that if I can show a person how to resolve the obvious problem, I have taught him the process that will enable him to deal with the problem that this one uncovers. I am interested in teaching a person the process of getting victory over defeat. If he learns it in one situation, maybe it will help him in the second and third. Then he can go on from there himself.

Of course, I am making room for God's power in a person's life. Insight helps. What good does self-understanding do? I have helped people become much more miserable because they understand themselves better. If they will not repent, then that is as far as I can go. Sometimes I have watched people walk out of my office with tears flowing down their cheeks. Because of me? No, I do not believe it for a minute. They must first deal with their rebellion. I cannot forgive sins. God does that. If you have defined a problem within a half an hour but the counselee does not like it and wants to spend another half and hour talking you out of it, you are wasting your half hour. This is when you may seem harsh, and you want to be sure that you are not. Was it not awful for the Lord to send that poor young fellow away suffering? Why did He not call him back and plead with him?

Prayer

I hesitate to say it, but I seldom pray with anybody. However, I do pray *for* them. I also tell them what to pray for. In my own opinion, a personal prayer is closet work. People must get in touch with God themselves. I am not the mediator. I am not a priest. I may help someone to clarify their problem, but I seldom pray with them.

People come to me with a problem that is "too tough for God." They have tried everything. I say right off the bat, "Look, you have not tried everything." Many problems people face involve a personal encounter with God. A woman who came to me one day who had seen me twice before with stomach trouble. She had crying spells and so on. I was able to take God's Word and help her see her sinful heart. She was a fervent church worker, a prayer warrior. I sent her home to meet God on the basis of her own sin. I have seen this many times. People come back radiantly happy. One said, "I have not cried for five days." Why not? "I have found the peace of God."

I do not beg and plead and agonize with people. I try to help them describe the problem and see their sin. The rest is beyond me. It takes faith to talk about personal sin to Christian people, prayer warriors, missionaries, and preachers. We have given lip service to sin but then we go looking for psychological problems.

Where to Turn for Self-Help

Everyone alive must deal with what the Bible calls the acts of the sinful nature. Everyone is driven to respond to the world around us in a way that the Bible calls the fruit of the Spirit.

Jesus said to His disciples:

"Peace I leave with you, My peace I give to you; not as the world gives."

John 14:27

The apostle Paul taught:

Live by the Spirit, and you will not gratify the desires of the sinful nature.

Gal. 5:16, NIV

Everyone has two options: to turn to God for help, or to turn to the world for help. It's like determining if you are headed north or south. Those are opposite directions.

Suppose we call heading Godward "north" and looking to the world "south." What help is there if you are headed south? You can turn for help to psychologically or psychiatrically trained people. These disciplines declare by faith that there is no God. We must help ourselves. There is a good deal of help in the world that allows the individual to find blessed relief from the effects of the sinful nature. Skilled therapists can help you channel the energy of the sinful nature into constructive ways. There are also many ways that the individual can find self-help.

Exercise

Golf courses, tennis courts, paddle, racquet, and handball courts, swimming pools, running tracks, bicycle and hiking paths, various kinds of health clubs, water skiing, snow skiing, bowling alleys are available everywhere.

Anyone who lives heartily, joyously, and happily, who is calm, still, and quiet should have some kind of exercise program to keep the body in shape.

This is clearly not the same as a person who has an exercise program in order to work off tensions, restlessness, and anxiety; or one who exercises to find relief from mental, emotional, and bodily stresses and strains.

Muscle Relaxation

Many high schools, colleges, and professionals offer study courses that teach us how to relax our muscles from head to toe.

Recently, I watched a television program that featured a Hindu swami giving a relaxation demonstration. He sat for fifteen minutes without moving a muscle while an announcer described the philosophy behind what the swami was doing.

Many years ago, I worked for a maternal health foundation. We had a division that pioneered in the field of teaching pregnant women how to relax during pregnancy and childbirth. The program worked wonders. This is now common practice all over the country. Multiplied thousands of women are grateful for such help which gives them a more comfortable, less painful pregnancy.

Quiet Activity

There is an endless supply of books available on every conceivable subject. We can lose ourselves by watching television or listening to music.

There are hundreds of table games available, an endless variety of hobbies, many college and professional athletic teams to watch, and many varieties of entertainment.

Business

There is a kind of elation, joy, fascination, and pleasure that comes from working, promotions, making money, success, praise, use of a skill, meeting people, entertaining, romance, travel, civic or church work, and getting an education.

Change

We can remove ourselves from certain people, change jobs, change fields, move to another location, or run away from an unacceptable task.

There is private therapy and group therapy available that enables us to explore the mind and emotions. We can change our philosophy, our standards, and morals.

Multitudes today seek peace by living it up, asserting their independence, doing their own thing, discovering themselves.

Chemicals

We are a pill-popping society. We can buy drugs for every need. Thousands use hard drugs and alcohol. Shakespeare said, "Oh God! That men should put an enemy in their mouths to steal away their brains."

What a fascinating list of ways to deal with today's tension. Yes, it's a great world, with endless ways to find peace.

King Solomon, who is described in the Bible as the wisest and richest of men, wrote of his efforts to taste of everything life has to offer. He sampled wisdom, mirth and pleasure, wine and folly; he built houses, vineyards, orchards, and gardens. He had servants and maidens, silver and gold. The Book of Ecclesiastes contains twelve chapters describing his quest. He concluded:

> Then I looked on all the works that my hands had done and on the labor in which I had toiled; and indeed all was vanity and grasping for the wind. There was no profit under the sun.
>
> Eccl. 2:11

Sooner or later, all our efforts to find peace from this world turn to ashes. When we slow down or are trapped by circumstances and people, the tension, restlessness, anxiety, and frustration return.

The activities available to us can help relieve the effects of unpleasant feelings and negative emotions, but we cannot remove them. Multitudes of retired people will testify to that.

What is wrong with heading south? Many Christians are on that road. Relief is relief wherever you find it. That is true. The relief that the world gives seems interchangeable with the relief God gives. Be advised that the source is not the same.

How to Tap God's Peace

There is a deeper kind of peace than that which simply relieves body and mind. It comes when you yield yourself to God and let His peace invade your soul. At various times, Jesus said:

> "Come to Me, all you who labor and are heavy laden, and I will give you rest. Take My yoke upon you and learn from Me, for I am gentle and lowly in heart, and you will find rest for your souls."
>
> Matt. 11:28–29

The apostle Paul, too, points us to God's peace.

> Now may the God of hope fill you with all joy and peace in believing, that you may abound in hope by the power of the Holy Spirit.
>
> Rom. 15:13

> Be anxious for nothing, but in everything by prayer and supplication, with thanksgiving let your requests be made known to God; and the peace of God, which surpasses all understading, will guard your hearts and minds through Christ Jesus.
>
> Phil. 4:6–7

Strengthened with all might, according to His glorious power, for all patience and longsuffering with joy.

Col. 1:11

King David, also one of the wisest of all men, learned of God's advice:

Cease striving and know that I am God.

Ps. 46:10, NASB

How do you approach God? Jesus said about Himself:

"I am the way, the truth and the life. No one comes to the Father except through Me."

John 14:6

"Behold, I stand at the door and knock. If anyone hears My voice and opens the door, I will come in to him and dine with him, and he with Me."

Rev. 3:20

Nicodemus was a ruler of the Jews. You can read an account of him in John 3. This man came to Jesus one night and said to Him:

"Rabbi, we know that You are a teacher come from God; for no one can do these signs that You do unless God is with him," Jesus answered and said to him, "Most assuredly, I say to you, unless one is born again, he cannot see the kingdom of God."

John 3:2–3

"For God so loved the world that He gave His only begotten Son, that whoever believes in Him should not perish but have everlasting life."

John 3:16

We stumble over the simplicity of this step. You are born again (or saved) when you believe Jesus. He said that you have access to the peace of God through Him.

231

The starting point is when you ask Him to invade your life—when you open the door and invite Him in. Jesus said: "I will come in." You either can or cannot point to a moment in your life when you made that decision.

Yesterday, I proposed this step to a disturbed counselee. He became more disturbed.

"Don't hand me that stuff," he said. "I've asked God for help many times, and it doesn't work."

"When did you ask Him to come into your life?" I asked.

"I've been a Christian all my life," he said. "I grew up in church."

I persisted. "When did you ask Him to come into your life?"

"I can't remember," he said.

To clarify this step to him, I asked if he remembered when he purchased his last car. That he could remember. He also remembered exactly when he got married, and when he accepted airplane tickets for his last flight, when he accepted his present job.

You are born again when you ask Jesus to invade your life. Otherwise, it's no deal. Jesus gives you access to God's resources: peace, joy, hope, patience.

Then you can put everything and everyone into His hands. You need not be in a dither over anything. You can stop striving and let His peace guard your heart, mind, and body.

It does not follow that, because you have access to strength from God, you will give Him your troubles, injustices, hatreds, hostility, conflicts, ill will. You can, but you can also nurse them within your body.

The biblical counselor, then, will refer a counselee to a clinically trained person or to a physician if the person has rejected turning to God and has chosen to live with the sinful nature—and has turned to the world for help.

It is important to note that the acts of the sinful nature are not beyond God's ability to heal. Nor are these acts beyond the biblical counselor's level of competency. If you want God's help, you turn north, you have access to His resources. Then the biblical counselor can help. If you turn south, you put yourself in the world's hands.

We are not talking about competence. We are talking about unrelated disciplines. In which will you put your trust?

◆

Appendix: Listening Sheet

Name _____

Address _____

Phone _____

Work Phone _____

Date _____

Follow-Up date _____

Notes (about what they said): _____

_____

_____

_____

_____

Statements (I made) Also, list Bibles verses I used:

_____

_____

_____

_____

Assignments:

1. _____

2. _____